WTF?!
What the French

WTF?!

What the French

OLIVIER MAGNY

NEW AMERICAN LIBRARY
New York

NEW AMERICAN LIBRARY
Published by Berkley
An imprint of Penguin Random House LLC
375 Hudson Street, New York, New York 10014

Library of Congress Cataloging-in-Publication Data

Names: Magny, Olivier, author.
Title: WTF?!: What the French/Olivier Magny.
Description: New York: Berkeley Books, an imprint of Penguin Random House, 2016.
Identifiers: LCCN 2016011036 (print) | LCCN 2016026078 (ebook) | ISBN 9780425283479 (paperback) | ISBN 9780698410237 (ebook)
Subjects: LCSH: France—Social life and customs—21st century—Humor. | BISAC: HUMOR/General. | HISTORY/Europe/France. | HISTORY/Social History.
Classification: LCC DC33.9 .M34 2016 (print) | LCC DC33.9 (ebook) | DDC 944—dc23
LC record available at https://lccn.loc.gov/2016011036

First Edition: October 2016

Printed in the United States of America
1   3   5   7   9   10   8   6   4   2

Cover design by Adam Auerbach
Book design by Kelly Lipovich

To the people of France.
Affectueusement!
OM

CONTENTS

ACKNOWLEDGMENTS

Dealing with French people on a daily basis is no piece of cake. Dealing with this Frenchman even less so. For this, my deepest gratitude goes to my formidable, patient, and beautiful wife.

Thank you to my ever-enduring parents. Thank you also to my in-laws for treating me like a son, despite my Frenchness!

Special thanks also to all the team at O Chateau and Caves du Louvre, and particularly to the captain of the ship: Nicolas Paradis.

Special thanks to my friend Cameron for his support throughout the writing of this book.

Thank you also to my agent Irene Goodman, who made this book possible. Her love of France and kind lenience with my silly texts have been a source of encouragement and joy. Thank you to Allison Janice at Berkley for editing out some of my silliest thoughts. Thank you also to Emmanuelle Heurtebize, who made this whole adventure possible.

Finally, thank you also to you, dear reader, for picking up this book. It is nice to think that there is someone on the other side of these words.

WTF?!
What the French

INTRODUCTION

$\mathcal{T}$he story of this book started a few years ago when I started writing a blog for my wine-tasting company. The blog was called *Stuff Parisians Like*. Much to my surprise, the blog grew quite popular and soon enough became a beautiful little book. I would have been happy with the story ending there.

It did not.

In just a few weeks, the book became a bestseller in France. I suddenly started to receive extremely incongruous notes: one from a student telling me their professor at La Sorbonne had them study two of my texts in class, another one from a theatrical director who asked me for permission to read and act out my silly writings onstage. Snail mail also got more interesting, as I received translations of my book in Polish, German—heck, even Taiwanese!

The day you receive your book in Taiwanese is a strange one. Especially when your day-to-day is absolutely not that of a writer. In real life, I'm an entrepreneur. At age twenty-three, I started a wine-tasting company. The following decade of my life I dedicated to trying to make French wine, and somehow French culture, more intelligible to the clients of O Chateau. Many fascinating discussions, much hilarity, and countless glasses of wine ensued.

This new book is the continuation of these discussions. I'm afraid you'll have to pour your own vino, but I hope you find in the following pages a story you'll find interesting, possibly helpful, and at times amusing. My ambition was never to write a book that would be comprehensive about any of the aspects I touch on. Even though it is sourced, fact-checked, and documented; even though it was written by someone who's 100 percent French, who grew up in France, and who has started and operated a business in France, this is not a guidebook, a manual, or a textbook—it is more of a snapshot. I tried to angle the lens and shoot from a distance that I think will help you gain a better understanding of France through all of the realities, facts, trends, and quirks this book describes. I'm sure you'll have your share of surprises.

Now, get that glass of wine, kick back, and enjoy!

LE TERROIR

$\mathscr{U}$nderstanding France—and wine while you're at it—requires being acquainted with a word the French language had the elegance to give birth to and to nurture. That word is *terroir.*

Ask a wine lover what makes a great bottle of wine so great: *le terroir.* Why is this winemaker so excited about this small little parcel on that particular hill? *Le terroir.* What is so wonderful about Burgundy or Piemonte? *Le terroir. Le terroir* is somewhereness; it is the essence of a place, its signature. It is what's unique, nonreproducible, and singular about it.

In the world of wine, this translates into the unique combination of soil, subsoil, climate, topology, etc., all of which contribute to giving a unique taste to the grapes and therefore ultimately to the wine produced in that particular place. French wine is so complex and diverse because, to the very core of how it is organized, farmed, and sold, it values terroir. In France, names of places—not of grapes—define wine. People in France order Bordeaux, Beaujolais, Sancerre, and Champagne, which are all regions, not Merlot, Pinot Noir, or Sauvignon Blanc, which all refer to grape varieties! Wine, for the French, is about where it's from far more than about what grape(s) it's made from.

Ultimately, terroir is what makes one place different from another.

The terroir of the American South at the beginning of the last century gave us jazz, just like that of the Bronx in the 1980s gave us hip-hop.

France is home to countless terroirs, which have been shaped over millennia. It is also home to a culture that recognizes, appreciates, and sometimes even reveres them. Anyone who has traveled extensively through France can grasp the tremendous variety in architecture, cuisine, wine, accents, crops, sports, and cultural references from one French region to the next. Normandy is immediately and irremediably distinguishable from Alsace, in the same way that Provence is different from Brittany, or Corsica from the Alps.

Most French people are gourmands, so when they travel to these regions, they have high expectations. Go to Normandy and your intake of Calvados and cider will automatically increase. Visit Brittany and crêpes will be your *passage obligé*. Head to Marseille: bouillabaisse and rosé wine will most likely be on the menu. Off to Alsace? You'd miss out by not sipping Alsatian wine or beer while enjoying a good choucroute.

While the expression of terroir in the world of wine—since it is complex, extremely varied, and thus requires some getting acquainted with—makes many people consider French wine as "too complicated," visiting France shows how wonderfully diverse, tasty, and unpretentious the culture of terroir truly is.

In a global world that threatens to obliterate differences, recognizing, appreciating, and seeking expressions of terroir—whether in wine, food, music, architecture, or language—are the ticket to a more delectable and richer life. If wine has one thing to teach us, it really is the beauty and value of *le terroir*. For while the word is French, the reality is not. Terroirs are everywhere. So come along, dear reader, and join the joyful bunch known as the terroirists!

Useful tip: If you want to experience wines that express their terroir the most, ask for "biodynamic" wines at your local wine store.

Sound like a French person: *"L'amour du terroir, c'est important quand même dans la culture française."* (The love of terroir—it's actually an important part of French culture.)

L'APÉRO

There is no understanding French culture without understanding the paramount importance of *l'apéritif.*

L'apéritif is the moment preceding a meal when drinks and finger food are consumed. It's the warm-up, the buildup, the foreplay before a meal. In and of itself, the mere existence of the concept of drinks and food before drinks and food should suffice to guarantee an irrevocable spot for France in the hall of fame of the world's greatest nations.

The *apéritif* is an absolute landmark of French culture—and is typically referred to by its familiar nickname *l'apéro.* It is essential to realize that even though food can be served, *l'apéro* is really about the drinking. Heck, French supermarkets even have a section of the drinks aisle called *apéritifs,* where all the traditional *apéro* drinks are gathered.

Meals in France are a serious matter—you should ease into them. *L'apéro* is that buffer between the harshness of nonmeal life and the pleasant parenthetical that a proper French meal should be. It is about transitioning to your more relaxed, more social, and more joyful self.

Prendre l'apéro is more about sharing a moment than just having a drink. It's about taking the time to do it. So the first thing your server should ask after you are seated at a French restaurant is: *"Un apéritif pour commencer?"* That is one legitimate question!

It is essential to pick up signals when it comes to the *apéro* culture. If a friend offers you an *apéritif* for lunch on a weekday, the plan is clear: boozy lunch. Not much solid work is going to be achieved that afternoon. At night, *apéros* can be had solo at home to take the edge off, or with friends or colleagues, or at a bar. Girls like to have *un p'tit apéro entre filles* (a girls-only *apéro*), while guys typically prefer *un apéro entre mecs* (a guys-only *apéro*). What is served depends on social class, trends, regions, and seasons. During spring and summer, *apéro* rhymes with *rosé*.

Go to the South of France and pastis (and its derivatives like maur-esque) will be your go-to *apéro* drink. In Burgundy, kir (black currant liqueur mixed with white wine) is the traditional choice. Climb the social ladder and *l'apéritif* is equated with Champagne. Head to Mar-tinique, Guadeloupe, or Réunion Island and rum will dominate the scene. Foodwise, anything could potentially be on offer, from sad little *caca-houètes* (peanuts) all the way to fancy *amuse-bouches*. The most common option is simply *gâteaux apéritif*—think a better, more eclectic version of crackers (which undoubtedly constitute another very French section of local supermarkets). Every French person is highly familiar with the few typical *gâteaux apéritif*, and everyone has a favorite (e.g., *les Curly*, *les Tucs*, etc.).

When French people have friends or family over, *l'apéritif* is an es-sential part of the event. It is not held at the dinner table and requires a separate venue (outside, on the sofa, by the coffee table, etc.). Only once *l'apéro* is finished (and the food is ready) will guests be asked to sit down for the meal.

L'apéro is such a pleasant time of any French social experience that it has morphed into an experience in and of itself. It went independent! Over the past few years, *l'apéro* stopped simply preceding meals and started to frequently supplant them.

L'apéritif dînatoire was born: no formal dinner, but enough food to satisfy all guests. Many corporate events or family affairs now take the form of more flexible and mingly *apéritifs dînatoires*.

But the real fun in the new, reinvented world of *apéritifs* is to be had by the younger crowd. Younger French people don't do dinner parties as much as their elders, frequently lacking the time, space, money, desire, or cooking skills. Yet they love to meet up for *un apéro*. There is something very open and noncommittal about it that fits the Millennial lifestyle. The invitation implies that everyone can leave early or invite friends. It also implies that things can get wild and go all night if the vibe is right. No definite script. The atmosphere is usually more relaxed than more formal social functions, so *apéros* tend to be great fun and may end up lasting even longer than your good old traditional French meal. Incorrigible Frenchies!

Useful tip: Always bring a bottle of wine. Not too fancy.

Sound like a French person: *"On fait un apéro vendredi soir. Tu veux passer?"* (We're having an *apéro* Friday night. Wanna stop by?)

FRENCH DANCING

$\mathcal{Y}$ou may be surprised to find that there is such a thing as French dancing.

It can be summed up in two words: bad dancing.

In France, dancing is about acknowledging the music. Following it is secondary. Who's that good at dancing anyway? In France, just getting your body in motion will qualify you as an utterly fun person. A French party animal is just someone that moves some body parts when she hears music. Coordination is irrelevant. It is quite okay to look bad. It is actually okay to look like you might—just possibly—suffer from some mild and heretofore discreet mental affliction. The French are open-minded like that. Here, there is always a mild feeling of relief when the music stops and people get back to normal: they were not impaired; they were just French!

Now, while the majority of French people specialize in erratic motions, some step it up a notch. On the dance floor, these ones do not look like they might have a disease; they just suck. When it comes to dance skills, plain sucking will make you one of the best dancers in France. No questions asked. You're a natural.

French dancing is primarily arm dancing. Sooner or later, French dancing will provide the observer with the ultimate French dance move: the arms-up move. When the chorus of a song comes up, 80 percent of the people on the dance floor will raise their arms to the sky—again, most likely not in time with the music. For the most energetic people or the greatest tunes, their bodies will follow their arms skyward and then their feet toward the ground. The French will start jumping along with the music.

That moment is the peak of a French party. If your guests leave without jumping with their arms up in the air, the party—no matter what the guests may say—was just a little underwhelming. A party climax in France is all about the jumping.

Extra cool points will be scored by those raising only one arm. This tricky maneuver is typically employed by smokers or people holding a drink. Double score if you can hold both a cigarette and a drink while raising one or two arms. You are obviously incredibly coordinated and so, indeed, just plain cool.

Some social groups have decided not to let their Frenchness deter them from owning the dance floors. As such, they have specialized in a specific type of dancing, which incidentally will give them away immediately. Here are a few of these other types of dancing *à la française*:

- Dance *le rock* and you are no doubt about it *un bourge*—spawn of the dying breed known as the proper French Catholic bourgeoisie. Rock dancing can be fun and sometimes impressive to watch. Usually, however, even when fully mastered, it is rendered with no rhythm whatsoever. Mechanical masterpiece, groove tragedy.

- Dance *la tectonique* and you'll be viewed as *un jeune*—a youngster. Older people will lament that, in their day, you didn't dance on your own; you had a companion. Young adults will look down on you for mastering something they don't, and that reminds them they're no longer on the cutting edge. They will try to bust one or two moves, jokingly. French soft hilarity typically ensues.

- Dance *le hip-hop* and you're *une racaille*—a hoodlum. While twenty years ago outliers would *faire du modern-jazz,* now the new generation of young French girls *fait du hip-hop.* In all fairness, though, it should be noted that, thanks to the spread of hip-hop culture, France is home to some of the best hip-hop dancers in the world.

On the subject of dancing, one thing has become clear to most young French people: *Les Américaines, elles dansent comme des putes*—American girls dance like prostitutes. Young French boys will join in with awe and excitement evident on their faces, while French girls will offer some of the most disgusted-looking Gallic shrugs of your life. Contempt and jealousy combined will do that.

At that point, they'll go back to the dance floor acting like they'd rather be somewhere else.

Compared with many other cultures, the French culture does not grant a significant role to dancing. While many French girls take dance classes in their childhood and find dancing fun, most Frenchmen dread it. The dance floor at a typical French wedding will frequently be filled with women only. Occasionally, a few girls will try to drag their dates or husbands out of their chairs. Actual pulling will occur. Usually unsuccessfully.

Frenchmen prefer to stay seated and drink the night away with their buddies: *"J'aime pas danser. Putain, pourquoi elle m'emmerde?"* (I don't like dancing. Damn, why is she bugging me?)

Useful tip: If you are a good dancer and a woman, you will become the center of attention on any French dance floor.

Sound like a French person: *"Moi j'aime beaucoup danser mais avec Michel, c'est vrai que c'est pas tous les jours!"* (I love to dance, but with Michel, it's only once in a blue moon!)

BLOWING AIR

𝒜mong humans, most communication is nonverbal. Among French people, however, a fair bit of the nonverbal communication remains mouth-centric.

While unmistakably French mouth shrugs are a well-known Gallic trait, another essential mouth movement escapes the sagacity of most visitors and observers.

That movement consists of blowing air.

Short of an attentive study of the French air-blowing ways, foreigners will miss the bulk of the small refinements that make up the richness and depth of social interactions in France.

Several emotional states can be expressed much more conveniently through blowing air than by using words. Blowing air can mean a number of different things:

1. **"I'm impressed!"** To show that you are impressed, curve your mouth, both corners pulled downward (think sad smiley face). Keep your lips relaxed. Then push air out gently through the tips of your lips. Once. A small, lean sound will ensue. Accompany this sound and movement by a nod and/or chickenlike tilt. That, right there, is French for "Wow—that's amazing."

2. **"I have no idea."** French people typically have the answer to most questions. In the rare occurrence that they happen not to, they shall express it through air blowing. To achieve a nonverbal *Je ne sais pas*, repeat the movement explained above and add to it a concomitant shoulder shrug. Nothing more, nothing less.

3. **"I'm frustrated."** Acting frustrated being so quintessential to Frenchness, it is key to be able to recognize and communicate that state of mind efficiently. Fortunately, it is a piece of *gâteau*. The pattern is as follows: Inhale through your nose; then expel that breath through the mouth in a generous, continuous, louder-than-usual blow. Once this general frame is understood, small variations will open the doors to truly blending in. In order to capture or express the wide palette of the French forms of frustration, one must focus on two things: the level of intensity and the shape of the lips.

   If the frustration is mild, the blowing should be discreet and quiet. It accompanies disappointing or unpleasant news. *Marc is gonna be late again. Pff . . .* That move is typically directed at no one in particular. It has more to do with inner monologue than with deliberate communication. The person doing this disappointed iteration of "blowing" is usually hardly aware of it. It is often a habit that could be interpreted as evidence that this Frenchie feels she is being faced with yet another confirmation that, indeed, no matter what, life always ends up sucking.

   As the blowing gets louder, the person moves toward performance mode. Either to express strong disapproval or to seek an unlikely form of French bonding born out of a moment of shared frustration. *I want to share with you but not to the point of actually speaking with you.* For example, the line at a supermarket is not moving much. Start a loud blow, and as the air comes out, turn to other people in the line and shake your head—as you keep blowing. Instant French bonding. All sorts of French facial expressions will be directed your way in response, ranging from the sad face nod to the eyes-wide-open awkward smile. At that point, you are almost family. Control of one's lips is crucial to conveying the right message to your audience. The looser the lips are, the more likely the resulting sound will resemble the noise emitted by a horse. This is French nonverbal for "I can't believe this crap." On the other hand, if no leeway is given to the lips and the air gets released in a clean, controlled, and non-horselike fashion, that right there will reveal exasperation.

Air blowing is an accentuated phenomenon among two communities in France. Teenagers—who are generally exasperated by most things. And Parisians—who also are. Chances are that, after reading this line, most Parisians actually couldn't refrain from releasing a state-of-the-art horselike blow.

Now you know.

Useful tip: Don't try this at home.

Sound like a French person: "Prt." (Prt.)

FRENCH RAP

France has for some time been the second largest rap market in the world. The early nineties saw the takeoff of rap as a mainstream form of music, and through radio and TV stations targeting young people, rappers like MC Solaar, IAM, NTM, Doc Gynéco, or Le Secteur Ä brought rap to the French masses, especially the younger masses.

Regardless of the region or social class they grew up in, almost all French twenty- or thirtysomethings today can recognize and sing along to the rap hits of the mid-nineties. French rap did create the anthems of a generation.

Care to listen to some? Just look up these songs on YouTube:

"Pose ton gun" by Suprême NTM
"Ma Benz" by Suprême NTM featuring Lord Kossity
"Le bilan" by Nèg' Marrons
"L'amour du risque" by Fonky Family
"Gravé dans la roche" by Sniper

There is nothing more precious than attending a party and being offered the privilege of witnessing upper-class French kids sing along about fistfights, dealing drugs, and wanting to shoot cops in the ghetto. The mainstreaming of the margins really is a beautiful thing!

The interesting aspect of this massification of rap as an art form is that it gave not only a voice but also an ear to a certain sector of youth. The *banlieues* became more visible, more audible. Their struggle, their frustration, their anger, and their aspirations too became a part of the French cultural and social landscape. Rap acted as a link between one France and another.

At first, while mainstream American rap had taken a turn toward big cars, guns, drugs, money, and babes, French rap remained more engaged in denouncing social injustice. However, slowly but surely, things shifted and, just like its American counterpart, French youth too found itself bombarded with images and messages of big cars, guns, drugs, money, and babes. Elevating stuff. Check out the song *"Boulbi"* by Booba on YouTube to find out more.

Other lovely ideas started to sprinkle French rap songs, one of the most popular being hatred for France. In the French hood, hating France, the French, and sometimes more generally white people—and claiming it loud and clear in rap songs—will score you some cool points.

Needless to say, when millions of young people listen to such messages day in and day out, it shapes the future of a country just as significantly as any lessons in school. Thankfully enough, the Internet happened. On YouTube, rappers that the media (particularly Skyrock, which had become *the* main radio outlet for rap music in France) were not promoting started to have a voice and began to grow an audience. New names started to gain popularity. Their messages were different from what the radio had been blaring for almost two decades, closer to the more conscious messages that had previously been popular. French rap had become not an enlightened voice for underprivileged French citizens, but instead a tool used by a few to spread a culture of violence, idiocy, hatred, and low morals among youth. But now a new rap offer was on the market, promoted by rappers involved in the new Internet subculture not beholden to labels and advertising budgets.

Today, French rap is at a very interesting point with a genuine dichotomy slowly appearing: on the one hand, vile mainstream rap, pushed, supported, and funded by the mainstream media,[1] and on the other, a new generation of YouTube rappers, with hundreds of thousands of fans, rapping much more conscious and educated messages.

For some examples of this, just look these up on YouTube:

"Le loup dans la bergerie" by Zirko
"Don't Laïk" by Médine
"La rage" by Keny Arkana

Useful tip: Le rap in *"verlan"*—a form of *banlieue* argot that inverts the pronunciation of words—is referred to as *le peu-ra.*

Sound like a French person: "Oh, le rap, moi, ça me casse les oreilles!" (Oh, rap—I can't stand it! [Literally: It breaks my ears!])

---

1 Very interesting read: *L'effroyable imposture du rap,* by Mathias Cardet.

BEING SERIOUS

𝒶sk anyone who's been to France what they think of French people and most will soon enough use the word *sérieux* to describe them. This national trait takes two main forms:

- The inability to laugh out loud. Very few French people have the ability to burst out laughing. The act of laughing in France is generally measured and almost completely silent. A French person laughing typically resembles a person smiling while having a short outbreak of the hiccups. That's plenty fun for the French.

- Being quiet. Nothing horrifies a French person more than witnessing the noise level generated by a table of Americans in a French restaurant. Particularly if they're having fun. It is not uncommon for French people to whisper when out to dinner. *Ne pas déranger les gens*—not disturbing people—typically ranks pretty high on the objectives list of a French person going out.

Consequently, many foreigners view the French as cold. But the truth is, they are simply well trained. Your traditional French education is not one that cuts a lot of slack for a disruptive child. In most families, children are constantly reminded of the rules of *savoir-vivre*: *"Tiens-toi droit"* (Stand/sit up straight), *"Ne mets pas les coudes sur la table"* (Keep your elbows off the table), and *"Parle moins fort"* (Don't speak so loudly) are injunctions that most French children will have heard hundreds of times by the time they reach their teens. While American parents tend to favor the "It's okay, honey" or "Hey, buddy, why don't we try this instead?" approach, French parents typically stick to slightly drier versions: *"Ça suffit"* (That's enough) or *"Arrête"* (Stop) being the most common. Smooth operating!

Growing up in France means being constantly reminded of rules, limits, and boundaries. Typically by your parents, but occasionally the old adage "It takes a village" rings true and aunts, uncles, teachers, or even complete strangers chime in with *"Dis-donc, ça ne se fait pas, ça!"* (Hey, that's not done!). The result of this culture of high expectations for children, enforced without apology, is that children tend to be quieter, probably more well behaved, and not as out of control as they can be in other countries. A few years down the road, the result is a country filled with people frequently characterized by an obsessive adherence to rules, a common inability to relax and let go, and generally terrible moves on the dance floor!

Useful tip: If you're a loud laugher, keep it up! Most French people secretly envy you!

Sound like a French person: *"C'est un sale gosse, qu'est-ce qu'il est mal élevé!"* (What a little brat—such bad manners!)

LA RANDO AND LOOKING FLY

*F*renchly enough, the number one sport practiced in France is strolling.

Hiking, or *faire de la randonnée,* often shortened to *faire de la rando,* is a hobby that fifteen million French people indulge in regularly.[1]

The culture of strolling is deeply rooted in French culture. From the *promenade digestive* to the *promenade en famille,* the French like to walk around with no precise goal other than that of enjoying life. *"On va se balader?"* is an invitation frequently heard in France—one that can mean "Let's go for a walk" or even "Let's go on a trip somewhere." *Balades* and *promenades* are about wandering, enjoying the views, the fresh air, the sights, and the people watching.

Randonnées have more of a sporty undertone to them. While going for a *promenade* or a *balade* requires no special preparation or gear, *partir faire une rando*—going for a hike—typically requires planning, equipment, and minimal conditioning. France is home to countless options for the avid hiker. Close to ten thousand miles of trails offer a tremendous variety of options, with varying levels of difficulty. The

---

1 *"Les Français et la marche: le boom de la rando," France Inter,* July 22, 2013, www.franceinter.fr/ emission-le-zoom-de-la-redaction-les-francais-et-la-marche-le-boom-de-la-rando.

pantheon of the French *randonneur* is the GR20 in Corsica (*GR* stands for Chemin de Grandes Randonnées). It involves several days of strenuous hiking and stunning views in a common vacation spot for French hikers looking for a challenge.

The aging French population finds in *la rando* a great way to stay active while enjoying themselves at a minimal cost, although the growing popularity of the sport has led many to invest in gear. Sports gear chain Décathlon developed the Quechua brand for hikers. Over the past decade or so, millions of French people have started wearing Quechua products—*les vêtements techniques,* or technical clothing—which are perceived by most as good value and well designed. They started sporting Quechua shoes, Quechua jackets, Quechua backpacks . . . not only on their hikes but also in everyday life.[2]

Most French people who practice physical activity qualify as *sportifs du dimanche,* which is an ironic and demeaning term meaning "Sunday athletes"—i.e., not really fit, not really shooting for high performance, but still going out there, at least for an hour or two on Sunday. Weekend-warrior types. Most *sportifs du dimanche* like to discreetly tell the world about their sportiness.

Ultimately, wearing Quechua gear is very modern French self-assertion: it's not only about sporting a convenient and inexpensive item of clothing; it's also about telling the world that you don't do fancy or over-the-top, that you don't care much for appearances, and that you're all in all a humble and outdoorsy person.

Maximal Frenchness achieved.

2 Edouard Laugier, *"Quechua by Décathlon: de la marque de distribution à la marque de fabrication,"* Le Nouvel Économiste, July 26, 2012, www.lenouveleconomiste.fr/quechua-by-decathlon-15676/.

Useful tip: The surest way to identify a Frenchie traveling anywhere in the world? Look for that Quechua logo!

Sound like a French person: *"La rando, ça me fait un bien fou."* (Hiking does me so much good.)

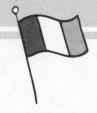

ÇA VA

❧

$\mathcal{F}$rench—some say—is a difficult language to learn. That is, if you forgo one essential rule: the generous usage of the phrase *Ça va* equates to fluency. Full mastery of this rule makes French speaking a remarkably approachable endeavor.

Ça va. Literally: "It goes."

SITUATION 1. A TYPICAL FRENCH CONVERSATION GOES AS FOLLOWS:

Salut, (insert first name), ça va? / Hey, X, how's it going?

Ça va, ça va, et toi? / Good, good, and you?

Ça va, tranquillement. Comment ça va au travail? / Pretty good, nothing special. How are things at work?

Oh ça va! / Okay, I guess. Don't really want to talk about it to tell you the truth!

Et la famille, ça va? / And how's your family?

Ça va, tout le monde va bien. / Yeah, everyone's good.

Et le travaux, ça va? / How's the construction going?

Ça va mieux! / Yes, it's going better!

SITUATION 2. SOMEBODY FALLS ON A SKI SLOPE. ANOTHER SKIER STOPS TO CHECK ON THE PERSON:

Ça va? /Are you okay?

Ça va! / I am. Thanks!

Sûr, ca va? / Are you sure?

Oui, oui, ça va, je crois. / Yes, thank you. I think I'm fine.

Et vos skis, ça va? / Are your skis broken?

Euh, oui, ça a l'air d'aller. / They seem to be fine.

Ça va is used just as commonly in the interrogative as it is in the affirmative form. One typically responds to the other. *Ça va* encompasses two families of questions, which in French would be *Est-ce que ça va?* and *Comment ça va?* Literally: "Does it go?" and "How does it go?" In other words, "Are you okay?" and "How are you doing?"

While extremely common, *Ça va* is far from being formal. When meeting someone for the first time or when you want to be polite, it's safer to go with *Comment allez-vous?*, which means the same thing but uses the polite "you" form *vous*.

Etymology being a cheeky thing, it teaches us that the phrase gained popularity in the French language in medieval times when the analysis of feces was an essential element to diagnose general health. *Comment allez-vous?* is ultimately but a mere reminiscence of the common medieval inquiry *Comment allez-vous à la selle?*

In that, the English language shares with French a similar scatological origin for its most traditional and polite of greetings: "How do you do?"

All things considered, sticking to the humble *Ça va* might really be the best thing to do.

Useful tip: With the right tone of voice and a hand gesture, *Ça va* can also be used as a sign that your patience has been exhausted!

Sound like a French person: *"Eh bah ça va pour lui!"* (Well, seems like he's doing well for himself!)

C'EST PAS POSSIBLE

*A*n old French saying asserts, *Impossible n'est pas français*—Impossible is not French. Combine effort, inspiration, faith, and panache with copious amounts of wine and you will find that most things in life are indeed possible.

However, these days, as the reality it describes is losing its accuracy, the phrase itself is losing traction in everyday conversations. Cognitive dissonance alert! Sadly, in today's France, most people have grown to internalize that "not possible" is ultimately far more likely than "possible."

France is clogged with an unfathomable number of rules, regulations, and bureaucratic nonsense, making everything that is not forbidden more or less mandatory. French freedom for you.

In a country where approximately half of the adults either work for the government or live off government subsidies, it should come as no surprise that the constant interaction with bureaucratic rules permeates everyday living.[1]

---

1 *"Part des fonctionnaires dans la population active,"* Observatoire des Gaspillages, October 9, 2014, www.observatoiredesgaspillages.com/2014/10/part-des-fonctionnaires-dans-la-population-active/.

Marc Lassort, *"France: le vrai taux de chômage est de 21,1 percent!,"* IREF, June 14, 2015, http://fr.irefeurope.org/France-le-vrai-taux-de-chomage-est-de-21,1,a3388.

Any expat who has interacted with *l'administration* will be hard-pressed to keep her love of France intact. It's a true test to that cute love affair! You do not know what wanting to bang your head against the wall, crying and screaming, means until you have dealt with the French bureaucracy. After you have waited for a few hours to be attended to by an agent, it is highly unlikely that you won't be missing a form, a signature, a stamp, or a relevant identification document. Life is smooth sailing until you try to obtain a document from a French government paper pusher. That paper will cost you some life points!

French people now know that there is probably a rule making what they are interested in, hoping, or trying to do if not illegal, then at least subject to authorization, a permit, taxation, or auditing. This makes the pursuit of any initiative somewhere between heroic and nonsensical (the line between the two being thin—always), and, in any case, exhausting.

As a consequence, the default answer most French people will give to any suggestion, idea, or request you present them with will be: *Non*. *Non*, typically followed by, *C'est pas possible*. By *C'est pas possible*, what the French person means is:

- There is a rule against that. Sorry.
- I'm not aware of any clear, direct rule pertaining to that subject matter, but in all likelihood, given the complex web of rules that characterizes this place, there is a good enough chance that there is one, and if not, I would have to juggle and justify so many loopholes to satisfy your request that just thinking of the endeavor and its possible repercussions is killing me and ultimately absolutely not worth my time, risk, or effort.

Most French people have grown to be fine with most things being *pas possible*. The phrase is now so prevalent that it is pervasive in situations where you would least expect it:

French bouncers will typically turn down patrons they don't want to see in their club with the phrase: *"Désolé, ça va pas être possible!"* (Sorry—can't let you in!)

A group of girls making fun of someone's attire or general looks: *"Sérieusement, c'est pas possible là!"* (Seriously, is she kidding with that look?)

A mother on the verge of a nervous breakdown: *"C'est pas possible—j'en peux plus!"* (I can't take it anymore!)

A man complaining about someone's stupidity: *"C'est pas possible d'être aussi con!"* (It's impossible to be that stupid!)

A girl complaining about a colleague she can't stand: *"Non, mais lui, c'est juste pas possible!"* (I can't stand that guy!)

Liberté, égalité, impossibilité.

Useful tip: If I've written three books, you can be sure that anything's possible!

Sound like a French person: *"C'est pas possible d'être aussi vulgaire que cette fille."* (This girl is as vulgar as they come.)

BEAUTY

$\mathcal{T}$he joke goes that God created France, the most beautiful country in the world with so much good in it, and ended up feeling guilty about it. He had to do something to make it fair. And so, he created the French people.

France is indeed blessed with breathtaking beauty. From the charm of an Alsatian village to the epic coastline of Brittany, from the majestic Alps to the vine-covered *garrigue* of the Languedoc, beauty is so common in France that, after a while, it becomes easy to get used to it.

While in many countries encountering beauty requires driving to a well-known highlight to find oneself amazed by a monument or a natural landmark, in France chances are the drive might be just as enjoyable. There is something soothing about getting mildly lost on the roads of France. The French countryside—*le plus grand jardin du monde* (the largest garden in the world)—is constant eye and soul candy. For generations, French peasants have been working this land, shaping it, clearing it, planting it, working it, caring for it. The French word *paysan*, from which *peasant* derives, attests to, that intricate link between the French people and their land. The *paysan* (who today would be—less poetically—referred to as the *exploitant agricole*) is the man who makes the *pays* (the country). The hard work and the humility of generations designed a country where natural beauty responds to charming architecture, where functionality somehow repeatedly managed to lead to grace and beauty.

The fact that France is also home—in what is ultimately a relatively small country—to a mind-boggling variety of climates and topologies surely doesn't hurt. Whether you're drawn to beautiful beaches, mountains, hills, plains, lakes, rivers, cold water or warm water, dry weather or wet weather, arid vegetation or lush forests . . . if you're interested in one particular type of beauty, chances are France has it somewhere. The natural beauty the country offers is an endearing complement to the architectural beauty of France, shaped by centuries of making beauty a cardinal element of a life well lived.

As time has passed, however, the deeply rooted cultural and physical attachment the French feel to their soil, to their region of origin, and to their heritage may not be as prevalent in everyday life as it used to be. But to this day, that gift of Nature manifests itself through the variety of wines, cheeses, and cuisines that characterize France. Even more beauty, you impossible little devil of a country.

France is home to many UNESCO World Heritage sites, but France has also created its own label to celebrate its own beauty. To that end, the organization *Les Plus Beaux Villages de France* is a terrific resource that brings together the many breathtaking villages that sprinkle the French territory.

Since by now you and I have developed a bit of a relationship, let me take the liberty of sharing some of my favorite beautiful places in France:

NORTH: Cap Blanc-Nez, Baie de Somme, Vieux-Lille, Gerberoy, Parfondeval

NEAR PARIS: The gardens of the Château de Versailles, Giverny, Forêt and Château de Fontainebleau, Château de

Pierrefonds, Barbizon, Château de Chantilly, La Roche-Guyon, Provins, Château de Vaux-le-Vicomte . . . and Paris, of course

WEST: The Étretat cliffs, Mont Saint-Michel, Presqu'île de Crozon, Baie de Morlaix, Pointe du Raz, Île de Bréhat, Ouessant, Cap Fréhel, Belle-Île-en-Mer, Le Bocage Normand, Saint-Malo, Honfleur, Locronan

EAST: Cascades des Tufs, Lac de Chalain, Alsatian villages and towns (Kaysersberg, Riquewihr, Eguisheim, Colmar), Grotte d'Osselle, Lac des Rousses, Lac de Lispach, Cascades du Hérisson, Plateau des Mille Étangs

ALPS: Mont Aiguille, Lac d'Allos, Mer de Glace, Lac d'Annecy, Grottes de la Balme, Parc du Mercantour, Mont Blanc, Lac du Pontet, Yvoire, La Grave

CENTER: Volcans d'Auvergne, Méandre de Queuille, Apremont-sur-Allier, Gargilesse-Dampierre, Charroux

SOUTH/SOUTHWEST: Cirque de Gavarnie, Orgues d'Ille-sur-Têt, Gorges du Tarn, Gorges de l'Ardèche, Marais du Vigueirat, Dune du Pilat, Lac du Salagou, Courant d'Huchet, Bassin d'Arcachon, Canal du Midi, Carcassonne, Brantôme, Cap Ferret, Saint-Étienne-de-Baïgorry, Collioure, Sare

SOUTHEAST: Plateau de Valensole, Lac de Sainte-Croix, Ocres de Rustrel, Calanques de Cassis, Gassin, Sainte-Agnès, Lourmarin, Seillans, Roque-sur-Cèze

CORSICA: The Bonifacio cliffs, Désert des Agriates, Îles Lavezzi, Porto-Vecchio, Piana, Sant'Antonino

DOM/TOM (FRANCE OVERSEAS TERRITORIES): Bora Bora (Tahiti), Île des Pins (New Caledonia), Cascade de Grand-Galet (Réunion Island), Piton de la Fournaise (Réunion Island), Hell-Bourg (Réunion Island)

Useful tip: Get off the freeway.

Sound like a French person: *"Les enfants, regardez comme c'est beau !"* (Kids, looks how beautiful it is!)

FABRICE LUCHINI

$\mathcal{I}$n a few countries of the globe a man can earn a living reading poetry. Only in France, however, can a man turn a show that consists of reading poetry into a proper pop culture hit. That man is Fabrice Luchini.

Very few people in France have a neutral opinion when it comes to "Luchini." Some find him brilliant and others call him annoying, but most recognize that he can be entertaining and sometimes straight up hilarious.

Who is Fabrice Luchini? All at once a self-taught expert in French literature, a former *garçon coiffeur*, a media darling, an actor, and a man who sits down in front of crowds to read and comment on excerpts of old books he admires.

Luchini's popularity stems from his many grandiose appearances on French television. In them, he speaks French in a way that very few still can. He manages to honor the language while quoting and referencing classic authors, talking about the delights and curses of the human condition, dropping in the occasional *verlan* word, and cracking jokes that make viewers think that, even though he's both well-read and well-spoken, he's one of them—ultimately a fellow human being.

Luchini is one of a kind. He can quote entire poems by Molière,

Baudelaire, or La Fontaine, and he can also quote Nietzsche or Beckett. In the next breath, he'll try to seduce the hostess or break out in a famous tune in the middle of a diatribe.

Over the years millions of French people have seen his shows, in which he appears onstage alone seated on a chair to read excerpts of *les grands auteurs.*

Luchini strikes in them a chord: his performance is a lasting tribute to a world where beautiful words, precise syntax, silences, and suggestions mattered. Somewhere between nostalgia for more delicate and well-spoken times, exploration of the implacable nature of the human experience, and vigorous invitation to aim higher and cut through the BS of modern society, *un spectacle de Luchini* is a rare moment of elegance, intelligence, poetry, and playfulness—undoubtedly a must for any French speaker lucky enough to get to catch one. For all the rest, YouTube is not a bad place to start to get to know the man and (as one should) develop an opinion about him.

Useful tip: If you speak a bit of French, look him up next time you're headed to France. You might be able to catch one of his shows.

Sound like a French person: *"Luchini, il est énorme!"* (Luchini's outstanding!)

NUDITY

$\mathcal{F}$rance does not have a puritanical tradition and so, culturally, nudity is fine.

Since antiquity, European artists have represented the human body naked. *Le nu* (the nude) is an artistic genre in and of itself, covering periods and movements including Impressionism, Rococo, Neoclassicism, Romanticism, Baroque, and so on. The naked body, while private, is not taboo. For centuries, its representation by artists has been the source of aesthetic, mental, and spiritual gratifications that go far beyond mere eroticism. Naked Adam and Eve, naked children or cherubs, naked women, naked goddesses . . . every French museum, every French château is filled with paintings featuring naked human bodies. As such, most French people grow up exposed to these works of art.

In fact, French people are never taught to turn their eyes away from nudity. Consequently, the sight of a reasonably healthy naked human, whether in a painting, a photograph, a movie, or in reality does not make French people particularly uncomfortable. A look at beaches on the French Riviera will immediately confirm this. Toplessness galore!

While your average French teenager may giggle at the sight of a naked body, he typically quickly gets over it. All the more so as nudity, which is a proven sales booster, is everywhere in France. Trying to sell shampoo? Throw in a naked person using it. Trying to sell perfume? Throw in a naked person apparently smelling good. Trying to sell cosmetics? Throw in a naked person with a luminous complexion . . .

For first-time visitors, walking French streets or watching French TV might feel like a rather risqué experience. French people do not necessarily notice that most of the windows of their pharmacies are covered with a rather incongruous number of ads presenting naked bodies—which could probably qualify as porn in the United States!

Most French people struggle to understand why many Brits, seeing a bare breast on TV, act disturbed and uncomfortable. The fact that many Americans act almost disgusted when unexpectedly faced with a bit of skin is entirely bewildering to most French people, whose reaction typically oscillates between neutrality and discreet joy.

Consequently, should you find yourself hitting a French changing room (such as at the swimming pool or gym), be prepared to see some skin . . . *à la française*, of course!

Useful tip: The adjective *risqué* in French simply means "risky," and does not come loaded with kinky connotations.

Sound like a French person: *"Et l'autre, il se balade à poil, tranquille."* (Look at that one, hanging out naked as if it's nothing.)

LE GOÛTER

*C*ompared with Americans, French people eat dinner late.

Compared with Spaniards, they eat it early.

With your typical French dinner starting between seven thirty and nine p.m., hunger kicks in at some point before dinner. This is traditionally dealt with in France with the loveliest of strategies: *le goûter.*

Le goûter could be called a snack. But realistically, in the French unconscious, the *goûter* is far more than just a snack.

First off, *le goûter* is not only something to eat; it's a time of day: *C'est l'heure du goûter*—It's snack time. A time of utter excitement, sometimes preceded by the heartbreaking words *Ce n'est pas l'heure du goûter* every time your parents turn you down when you ask them for something sweet in the middle of the day.

Le goûter is every French kid's favorite time of the day: four thirty p.m.—the bell rings. School is off for the day. Next step: feasting on something sweet. Now we're talking. Parents, siblings, nannies, and grandparents—whoever is in charge of picking up the kids from school—can implement different strategies at that point:

STRATEGY 1: On the way home, opening *un paquet de gâteaux* (a pack of cookies) and letting the famished child feast.

STRATEGY 2: Stopping at the boulangerie en route home to pick up your favorite *viennoiserie*: *croissant, pain au chocolat, pain au raisin, pâte à choux, pain au lait, brioche au sucre* . . . tough decisions. While you're at it, you'll also typically get the baguette for dinner.

STRATEGY 3: Bringing the *goûter* to the child, right outside the school's gate.

Needless to say, daily repetition of strategy 2 will turn any French kid into quite the connoisseur. Soon enough, pointing starts to happen: your typical six-year-old French kid doesn't just want a croissant; he wants *that* croissant. Nope, not that one—yup, that's the one—that's the good one! Yeaahhh!

Walk into a bakery at four thirty-five p.m. and throughout France you'll witness the same exact ballet of children with their book bags and adults with a few coins.

And systematically, after the *goûter* has been selected, and while the lady from the bakery hands you the goods, you'll hear the accompanying grown-up ask the child, *"Qu'est-ce qu'on dit?"* (What do we say?). Too eager to get his hands on the croissant, the kid will please everyone with a *"Merci"*—the final condition for the treat. Except in families with good manners, where the mother will usually respond with a *"Merciiiii . . . ?"* or *"Merci qui?,"* to which the kid will utter, *"Merci, madame."*

Well worth the effort.

Le goûter is an undying French tradition. It's a central element to the French food culture. One reason French people don't snack as much is because *le goûter* ritual exists. It is the unknown fourth wheel to the carriage of French eating.

For a French child, *le goûter* is such a prominent part of life that you don't get invited to a birthday party: you get invited to *un goûter d'anniversaire*!

Which of course takes feasting to a whole different level!

Useful tip: Surprise your French friend on her/his birthday. Prepare a *goûter d'anniversaire* for her/him. Major *retour en enfance* and genuine thankfulness guaranteed.

Sound like a French person: "*C'est bientôt l'heure du goûter, non?!*" (Is it *goûter* time already?)

LE GAUCHISME

To understand the predominant ideology that defines the way a people think, it is essential to look at who is dispensing formation and information. In today's France, where the Catholic Church, which at one time held great influence, has become inaudible, that means taking a look at the ideological inclinations of teachers and journalists. Those two categories are in charge of filling up the brains of French people.

Over the past few decades, an overwhelming majority of French teachers have leaned on the left side of the political chessboard. The figure of the *prof gauchiste* (leftist teacher) is one all French people have encountered a few times throughout their formative years (or those of their children): chin-strap beard, leather man purse over the shoulder. Those *profs soixante-huitards* (i.e., with the mentality of the May 1968 upheaval) thrive on ideas of class struggle, profit bashing, and mocking the Catholic religion. Most teachers who are not leftist are just left wing (a crucial distinction)—less hard-core, but in agreement with the values. French middle and high schools to that extent resemble watered-down left-wing indoctrination camps. For students having to endure the long-term one-sided ideological brainwash that is a leftist education, there is, however, one perk most await eagerly: the *jours de grève* (strike days), when a majority of teachers go on strike and class is canceled. These typically happen more than once a year and feel a little bit like leftist Christmas.

The other category directly in charge of teaching French people how and what to think is journalists. Most polls show that journalists overwhelmingly vote for the left. This phenomenon is only growing stronger as the younger generation of French journalists, unlike the previous one, is the product of the leftist *éducation nationale*. Journalists have grown recently to be even more despised than politicians in France. They are typically viewed as *chiens de garde* (guard dogs) of the system, as foot soldiers in charge of forcing a homogeneous unsavory message down the throats of the general public. French journalists rarely question, listen seldom, but judge a whole lot. They typically are the epitome of conformism and, sadly, usually consider themselves progressive and forward-thinking. On TV sets, any dissenting view—on any topic—will be sanctioned: interviewers will morph into prosecutors, interviewees into suspects. A recent poll in the top journalism school in France showed that no student there had voted for a right-wing party. Zero.[1] In a sociological environment deprived of genuine disagreements, the real exchange of ideas and arguments between opposing views magically become obsolete.

Teachers are directly in touch with social realities as they witness violence and deterioration and can see the situation getting worse year after year. Some are therefore waking up to the fact that blind leftism might not be the best way to prepare students to live in the real world. Consequently, French teachers are slowly starting to change the way they vote and—one might hope—teach. Journalists, on the other hand, often live in city centers and don't have to face the consequences of the policies and views they advocate. They deliberately choose not to debate

---

1 François Ruffin, *"Les journalistes à gauche toute: mais de quel système sont-ils donc censés être les chiens de garde?,"* *Atlantico*, April 14, 2012, www.atlantico.fr/decryptage/journalistes-gauche-toute -systeme-censes-etre-chiens-garde-presidentielle-cfj-celsa-francois-ruffin-330312.html.

with people with dissenting views and so stories continue to present a one-sided view of the issues facing the country. Anyone who disagrees with what the modern orthodoxy journalists regurgitate is commonly viewed as *facho* (fascist) and banned from any discussion. Intolerance in the name of tolerance. Welcome to the Orwellian world of French journalists.

In France, like anywhere else, people are born and educated with all sorts of political inclinations. The key, however, to understanding the French psyche these days is to realize that constant exposure to leftist messages since childhood comes with one essential consequence: the ideology pervades and other views are ignored or, worse, invalidated.

France is consequently home to many *gauchistes* (leftists). *Gauchistes* are the virtual superheroes of social interactions. They are the police of capitalism and they're out to get justice. *Gauchistes* are the bearers of the inalienable truth according to which evil capitalists are exploiting poor people and constantly taking advantage of them. Everywhere, all the time, end of story. There is no debating this. Start a business: you're an evil capitalist. Shut down the business: you're an evil capitalist. All companies are structures of exploitation in which an evil *patron* (boss) exploits kindhearted *exploités*. The facts that the job might be fulfilling, that the purpose of the company might be noble, or that the boss might make less money and have fewer vacation days than his employees are irrelevant.

It is virtually impossible to have a conversation with a French *gauchiste*. They are absolutists. They are right and you are wrong. This is all the more frustrating as this "left" is but a pseudo-left, neglecting in every way the poorest and most exposed. Try to evoke in a conversation the real power in our societies, and you'll be viewed suspiciously. Ask why the entirety of French income tax goes to pay the interest of the debt rather than to build hospitals and schools, and you'll be seen not as an educated and perceptive person but as a mildly deranged and suspicious character. Criticizing small-business owners: good. Asking why a private institution is in charge of printing the dollar: bad.[2] Try asking why work (which is all poor people have to offer to elevate their condition) is taxed more than capital, and once again you'll be viewed as a—you guessed it—*facho*! The main positive outcome of this double movement of radicalization and simplification of political discourse in France is that it shows that the concepts of left and right have become vastly meaningless in today's world.

However, leftism mentally pervades all French people, all the way to the right side of the political spectrum. The French *extrême droite* (extreme right) would undoubtedly be viewed as a left-leaning party in most countries on earth. When traveling to the United States, moderate "right-wing" French people invariably discover their inner left-wing Frenchie: all that mistrust for the government, wanting to have their own guns, and advocating total freedom of speech is really a bit dangerous . . . *Les Américains sont un peu extrêmes quand même!*

Useful tip: It is essential to make the difference between *être de gauche* and *être gauchiste*.

Sound like a French person: "*Un vrai gauchiste, complètement à l'ouest, le mec!*" (That guy's a true leftist—completely wack.)

2 On this topic, *The Secrets of the Federal Reserve* by Eustace Mullins is a must.

TAKING FLOWERS
SERIOUSLY

It is fair to state that many outdoor spaces in France are quite manicured. One of the key aspects of the lovely aesthetic of many French towns and villages is the attention to public vegetation. This attention is not only focused on the many parks France boasts, both national and local, but also on regular streets, avenues, and plazas.

France is home to approximately thirty-six thousand cities, towns, and villages—known in French as *communes*. Entering each of these municipalities comes with a few signs on the side of the road: one, mandatory, announces the name of the place, sometimes one will announce the time of Mass, and occasionally there will be one noting the town's sister cities elsewhere in the world (*villes jumelées*, or literally "twin" cities).

And then, in some small towns or villages, a uniquely French sign: one that announces just how beautiful the flowers look there—officially, in the form of a grade that acts as the sort of Michelin star of landscaping.

Who hands out such a ranking? Villes et Villages Fleuris de France is a pretty serious French institution. Twelve thousand of those thirty-six thousand French communes partake each year in its contest.[1] If

---

1 *"Le Conseil National des Villes et Villages Fleuris," Direction General des Entreprises,* November 10, 2014, www.entreprises.gouv.fr/tourisme/conseil-national-des-villes-et-villages-fleuris.

awarded, each commune may score one, two, three, or four flowers. *Les 4 fleurs* are the towns and villages judged to have the most beautiful flowers and vegetation filling their public spaces. There are major bragging rights when your town gets to plant that sign to welcome visitors. The BS-free sign clearly states the town's flower ranking and may bring secret joy to many French. However, if that village scored only one or two flowers, while their efforts are recognized and surely appreciated, they're expected to up their game next year!

While it may come across as a charmingly inconsequential prize, there is no doubt that having both elected officials and residents engaged in the beautification of their environment through flowers, plants, and trees adds tremendously to the quality of life of these communities. Caring for beauty may be under attack in France, but it is very far from being dead! The good news is, the communities that go that extra mile reap tremendous benefits in terms of tourism and image.

Not so silly after all!

Useful tip: Learn *le langage des fleurs* and make your flower gifting even more meaningful.

Sound like a French person: *"Tu as vu mes hortensias?"* (Have you seen my hydrangeas?)

DATING

$\mathcal{T}$raditionally, "dating" is neither a French term nor a French practice. The term got introduced into pop culture in the movie *La Vérité si je mens! 2*. This line from the film became famous and solidifies how foreign and mysterious the concept of dating is to French people:

> *Une date, ça veut dire: tu crois que tu vas niquer, mais en fait tu niques pas, c'est ça une date!* (A date means: you think you're gonna get laid, but actually you won't—that's what a date is.)

When it comes to courting, rules and codes are simply different in France. While things like asking someone out and going on the actual date are rather similar, the key differences lie in the *what happens after that part.*

Should you have an interest in dating a French person, the three following ground rules ought to be clarified:

1. As a general rule, French people don't date several people at once. Courting someone and going on a date means interest is already established. Accepting to go on a date means interest is there. Foreigners dating a French person for the first

time might perceive that person as rather needy or pushy after the first date. That is because the date was probably more meaningful and loaded with potential consequences for the French person in the first place.

2. Except in the case of utter drunkenness, kissing the other person on the mouth more or less establishes the start of a formal relationship. Should you kiss or be kissed by a French person, that is the unspoken understanding. Undoubtedly, it comes with setbacks, and also with perks! Once this is understood, it becomes essential to time that first kiss properly.

3. After dating for a few weeks, don't tell a French person that "you're ready to go exclusive." For that matter, don't tell that to *anyone* who's not American, for the whole concept of "going exclusive" after months of intimacy is viewed as an acceptable thing only in the United States. The other seven billion inhabitants of this planet will look at you thinking, "You mean we weren't already?" By French standards, the minute you kiss the other person on the mouth means you're exclusive.

In the digital age, the dating scene has changed significantly in France. Online dating has become a major phenomenon with sites like Meetic or AdopteUnMec. More recently the app Tinder has rendered the whole traditional concept of courtship laid out above vastly outdated for younger French people, especially in urban environments where the number of users (and therefore options) is much greater.

However, in a very French twist, some Tinder users have recently started using the one-night-stand app to search for true love. Twenty-first-century romance is an ever surprising quest.

Useful tip: Despite being French, the term *fiancé* is far more commonly used in English-speaking countries than in France.

Sound like a French person: *"Une de perdue, dix de retrouvées!"* (There are plenty of fish in the sea!)

BORDERS AND COUNTRY

*B*y definition, a country is characterized by the fact that it's controlled by its own government. The less legally inclined would add other attributes, such as controlling your own borders, having a currency of your own, an independent military . . . or, more important, a national soccer team.

Crossing a border is an exciting moment: the end of one world, the beginning of a new one. In Europe, however, borders have grown to become a thing of the past. Slowly but surely, crossing borders in and out of France became less and less memorable: little by little, no more customs officers, no more barriers. This situation has reached a point of complete underwhelmingness, whereby today, if you drive from France to Spain, you will no longer find a sign telling you that you've just arrived in a new country. Not one. The border has simply vanished. While it's still visible on world maps, the border between France and Spain (or Italy, or Germany . . .) no longer exists in the real world.

For a country to lose its borders is no small step in its history. Yet it happened so gradually, so smoothly, that most French people did not even realize it. While on paper removing some of the borders that separate humans does not sound like a bad idea, it is not the packaged narrative that was presented to Europeans over the years. The dominant narrative was: "Our country is too small. Look at the world: the U.S., Russia, China. We can't survive on our own; we need to be part of a bigger, stronger entity." Get big or die alone!

France is now a member state of the European Union. With the creation of the euro, it lost control of its monetary policy and of much of its budgetary policy. With the recent full-on return of France in NATO, France also vastly lost control of its military.

All in all, it is fair to say that France is now widely controlled by supranational entities (the EU, NATO, the ECB, etc.). Thankfully enough, it has preserved the most essential of country attributes: a soccer team!

Useful tip: Pierre Hillard is an accessible French scholar and world expert on the fascinating topic of globalism. Well worth looking up.

Sound like a French person: *"Au moins, tu ne risques pas d'avoir d'ennuis à la douane."* (At least you won't have any issues at customs.)

FRENCH VACATIONS

From an early age, the French learn that life is a succession of work and vacation, and that no matter how bad things are, vacations are at worst only a few weeks away. Throughout their school years, French youth get to enjoy sixteen weeks off per year. Broken down as follows:

- *Les vacances de la Toussaint* (All Saints)—one week in the fall
- *Les vacances de Noël* (Christmas)—two weeks in December
- *Les vacances d'hiver* (winter)—two weeks in February
- *Les vacances de Pâques* (Easter)—two weeks in April
- *Les grandes vacances* (summer)—nine weeks in July, August, and September

Graduating to being an adult means sacrificing some vacation time. However, with a minimum of five weeks' paid vacation per year, French employees have enough time off to build their lives around these guaranteed recurring oases of free time.

While the legal minimum is five weeks, on average French workers each year take 6.3 weeks off work. If you happen to work for the French government, it is not uncommon to enjoy more than seven weeks off per year (not including sick days).[1] For most French people, *les vacances* are eagerly awaited and planned with much attention.

When it comes to the subject of vacations in France, it is essential to grasp the notion of *vacances scolaires*, i.e., the sixteen weeks per year when school is off. For parents with a job, most *vacances scolaires* come with a problem: "I have to work. What am I going to do with my children?" During those times, grandparents, DVDs, and video games surely come in handy.

As with most serious things in France, vacations are regulated by the government. Those decisions have to be made at a national level—of course. Since giving time off to all French kids at the same time led to several inconveniences (excessive traffic, peak tourism, etc.), the decision was made long ago to split France into several "zones" in order to more efficiently schedule vacations throughout the year. When it comes to *vacances scolaires*, France is split into three distinct zones:

- **Zone A:** Bordeaux, Lyon, Burgundy, and the surrounding areas
- **Zone B:** Marseille, Nice, Normandy, Brittany, and the surrounding areas
- **Zone C:** Paris, Toulouse, and the surrounding areas

All French kids are sure to know which zone they are in so that they can determine when their next vacation will be. Each year, parents and children look with anticipation to see if the given vacation schedule will be advantageous or not: they don't want their vacations to overlap with bank holidays (which are obviously distinct from vacations—please don't be such a rookie). The whole family is quite bummed when a bank holiday happens to fall during *les vacances scolaires*. Lost paid vacation is definitely something to pout about in France.

---

1 Fabien Renou, *"Combien de congés en France? 6 semaines en moyenne,"* JDN, November 15, 2012, www.journaldunet.com/management/vie-personnelle/conges-en-france.shtml.

The concept of zones gives way to the peculiarly French phenomenon known as *le chassé-croisé des vacances* (the vacation crossover). Tourism destinations get successively filled by French people based on where they live. One week will be *la semaine des Parisiens,* the next *la semaine des Marseillais.* Intermediary weekends are moments of mad traffic on French roads. As one zone finishes their vacation period, another zone starts theirs.

Vacation coordination is an essential aspect of French life. Parents coordinate their vacation time with that of their children, friends make sure they take time off work at the same time, and cousins living in different zones have to be reunited on the few windows of opportunity the schedule gives. All French people manage their vacation time meticulously. "Okay, I'll take only five days for Easter, and this way I can take three weeks in August, and then maybe I'll take one day after that bank holiday, which is a Thursday this year, so *je fais le pont*"—that is, I'll get a four- or five-day weekend out of it by making a "bridge" of the one day off. Proper French social engineering.

When it comes to summer vacation, French society is split into two subcategories: *les juilletistes et les aoûtiens*—people who take their summer vacation in July and those who do so in August. The start of summer vacation (for both parents and children) gives way to *les jours de grands départs en vacances* (days of major vacation departures), or just *les jours de grands départs,* typically one in early July and one in early August. Needless to say, the last weekend of July gives way to epic traffic and monumentally French *chassé-croisé.* The cliché according to which many businesses in France shut down in August commonly holds true: with most of the staff being gone the first two weeks of August, the sound management decision is indeed frequently to close down the operation to make sure the loss of productivity is contained and circumscribed. When the domestic ecosystem is such that most other companies do the same, not much productivity is lost, since very little would get done during those weeks anyway.

Ultimately, whether for children, adults, or companies, vacation management is an essential part of French life, and one that comes with multiple headaches. Unsurprisingly, the French manage to create life complications out of being given copious amounts of time off.

Being French is exhausting.

Useful tip: To get the best deals on accommodations in France, avoid booking during *les vacances scolaires.*

Sound like a French person: *"J'ai posé quinze jours. J'suis crevé."* (I'm taking two weeks off. I'm spent.)

JE SUIS CHARLIE—
OR NOT?

"*You're* going to France. Aren't you scared?"

Five years ago, this question would have sounded hilarious. Scared of cheese, baguettes, and glorious wines maybe?

However, recently this question has become more common: things have changed. In 2015, France suffered two highly publicized terrorist attacks: *Charlie Hebdo* in January and the Paris shootings in November. After all the worldwide publicity, outrage, and compassionate digital outpourings of support from millions all over the world, it is safe to say that bread and cheese are no longer the only things that come to mind about France.

These attacks came as a gigantic surprise to most French people. It was not cartoonists or rock fans that had been attacked; to most French people, it was France and what France stood for.

The idea that people in France could be killed as a result of their political activism, their assumed religious beliefs (of lack thereof), or simply for being from a country whose government's actions don't appeal to some seemed not only egregious but truly unthinkable to most.

After the tragedies, most French people did not succumb to hatred, vengeance, or violence. They were surely aided in that by a media and political class that unanimously urged people not to jump to conclusions by pointing fingers at Muslims or Islam (France is home to millions of Muslims). In sum, the message was: *Pas d'amalgame*—Don't equate Islamist terrorism with all Muslims. Muslim radicals attacked France? The key priority becomes urging the French not to think or say (let alone do) anything negative against Muslims or Islam. In a formidably modern twist, Muslims had become the potential victims and French people the potential threat.

Amid fear, anger, and shock, analysis and ongoing discourse abounded. The argument according to which Muslim radicals account for only a small minority of the total Muslim population was one of the most commonly spread ones. Fraternal indeed, but some might say irrelevant, for in France, like in the rest of the world, even small percentages quickly add up to many thousands of radicals. Mathematics are annoying like that.

Atrocities were perpetrated and plunged France into incomprehension. Emotions took over, making the analysis of some of the incongruities in the official narrative almost impossible.

Unfortunately, the bad news for the French people did not stop with the death toll and the horror stories. The official discourse morphed: fighting terrorism meant fighting *les discours de haine* (hate speech). The authorities' battle in the war against *la haine* had started.

Week after week, irony and nuanced analyses lost ground in conversations, on- and off-line.

The peculiar concept of "Hatred" was to be sanctioned, public meetings were to be forbidden,[1] privacy was to be stomped, irony was to be reported, warrantless surveillance was to become the new normal[2] . . .

---

1 *"État d'urgence: le Conseil constitutionnel valide pour l'essentiel les perquisitions et interdictions de réunion,"* Le Figaro, February 2, 2016, www.lefigaro.fr/flash-actu/2016/02/19/97001 -20160219FILWWW00080-etat-d-urgence-les-perquisitions-et-interdictions-de-reunionvalidees -essentiellement-par-les-sages.php.

2 Kate Conger, "France Approves 'Big Brother' Surveillance Law," *Digital Trends*, July 27, 2015, www.digitaltrends.com/web/france-surveillance-big-brother/.

In a matter of months, the days of *"Je suis Charlie,"* the days of celebrating "freedom of speech," seemed long gone. It was as if a thick page had been turned, leading to a new ominous chapter in French history, one where even the highest-ranking officials in the French legal system took to the press to denounce the alarming drop in civil liberties and the fact that France's new legal apparatus paved the way for the establishment of a perfectly legal dictatorship.[3]

The tug-of-war between order and liberty is nothing new. Unfortunately, these days it seems as if the people of France are getting a bit of a bad deal, losing both ostensibly and at a fast pace. One thing's for sure, however: when wondering what the Orwellian war against "hate" and "terror" lead to, don't say "hate" or "terror," or you might get on the French government's *merde* list.

Useful tip: Don't forget to love.

Sound like a French person: "Tu vas être fiché, toi, avec tes conneries!" (You're gonna get on some government's watch list with all your shenanigans.)

---

3 *"Etat d'urgence: le bâtonnier de Paris déplore le 'recul de nos libertés publiques,'"* Le Monde, December 11, 2015, www.lemonde.fr/police-justice/article/2015/12/11/etat-d-urgence-le-batonnier-de-paris -deplore-le-recul-de-nos-libertes-publiques_4830199_1653578.html#xtor=RSS-3208.

Robin Panfili, *"En l'état actuel du texte, la France peut basculer dans la dictature en une semaine,"* Slate France, March 2, 2016, www.slate.fr/story/114869/sicard-justice-etat-urgence-decheance.

SPELLING

Wanting to learn French implies a certain degree of masochism. As if assigning a gender to each noun, organizing sentences with a complex web of grammatical checkpoints, making each plural a new adventure, and applying only seemingly steady rules to the world of conjugation—as if all this did not cut it—the French language decided to spice things up a bit by making spelling particularly challenging.

"Water" in French is one sound: *o.* Imagine the person who came up with that talking it through with a sane person:

It's pronounced *o*? Let's make that three letters!

> But it's just one sound, and it's water . . . should be pretty
> straightforward. Why do you need three letters?

Don't worry about it. Make it . . . hmm . . . let's see . . . *E* . . . *E*?
Yeah . . . man I'm on fire! *E* . . . *a* . . . ha! I'm loving this . . .
And . . . *u*! Ha—*u*! That is so good! *E-a-u: Eau.* Perfect. And
that shall be pronounced *o.*

> You're a psycho.

I'm a genius.

            So what about the plural? Just add an *s*?

Add an *s*? Who do you think I am? English? How can you lack
ambition like that? Have some panache for heaven's sake! Add an *x*!

            Pff . . . So *o* singular . . . *ox* plural?

Good Lord. Who raised you? Don't be so vulgar. Why would
you need to pronounce that *x*?

Some subject matters are simply more French than others. Spelling
is one of them. Discussions centered on spelling are surprisingly re-
current in France. (Who said, "How fun!"?)

French is a language of many unsettling asperities; their proper
command is to expression what good table manners are to dining. But
if the subject of spelling is frequently brought up in France, it is primarily because tragic spelling simply is a mere symptom of the dwindling command of French among French youth.

While two generations ago most people who did not go to university
had a near-perfect command of spelling, the French school system is now
spouting out illiterates by the tens of thousands each year. At age seven-
teen, a staggering 30 percent of French youth cannot even read properly.[1]
When a person struggles to merely read, let's just say that proper spelling
is not exactly on top of their priorities. Thinking that the remaining 70
percent are a bunch of Victor Hugos is somewhat illusory. When it comes
to proper French, undeniably the level has gone down. Big-time.

In fact, it is a massive understatement to say that, when it comes to
the command of French, the bar has been lowered dramatically in the
French school system. In a tragicomic turn, growing numbers of young
teachers with a poor command of their own language are starting to

---

1 Jean-Baptiste Noé, *"École: 30% d'illettrés en France," Contrepoints*, August 5, 2012, www.contrepoints
.org/2012/08/05/92831-30-dillettres-en-france.

teach French to children. The start of yet another vicious circle? Certainly not. The French regime came up with a new way to hide the collapse of its education system: dumbing down the spelling of the French language! In early 2016, a new reform was introduced to vastly rid the French language of the circumflex (^) accent, to turn *oignons* into *ognons*, and to ditch countless hyphenated words.

If you are learning French yourself, two things should boost your confidence.

1. You are not in the French school system. So your likelihood of one day having a good command of French is far superior than if you were learning French in the French school system.

2. Visit the comments section of any Web site geared toward young people in France and you will realize that not only is your spelling better than theirs, but so are probably your syntax and your grammar.

So even if your spoken French might not be as fluent as you'd like, chances are your written French is much better than that of millions of French people!

Useful tip: Google Translate.

Sound like a French person: *"Je sais jamais:* dilemme, *ça prend un* n *ou pas?!"* (I never know: is there an *n* in "dilemma"?!)

L'AGRESSIVITÉ

𝒯alk to French people living overseas and within five minutes you
will hear word for word:

> *En France, les gens sont hyper agressifs.* (In France, people are so
> aggressive.)

While certainly it is less true in the countryside than in the cities,
it is not an unfair statement.

The stress of modern life along with the anonymity of urban me-
tropolises surely contributes to explaining this phenomenon, but these
two factors do apply to most cities on earth. However, many French
people, it is true, do seem on edge these days.

Psychology shows that people get aggressive when they are stressed,
but also when they're tired, when they're pushed around, and when
they're in fear.

While most French people might not consciously acknowledge to
be living under these conditions, there is no doubt that, collectively,
France has been pushed around for a few decades and its people therefore understandably live in a constant state of anxiety. An aggressive
France is a suffering France.

In all fairness, a neutral analysis of the key changes of the past decades highlights the depth and brutality of the changes imposed on French society:

- Explosion of public debt to levels that can never be repaid and therefore plunge the country into debt slavery.

- Mass immigration, which has introduced new social and religious tensions for today and tomorrow.

- A shift away from traditional inherited Christian values toward a new set of socially acceptable values which are a 180 from the former, resulting in even more divisions.

- An explosion of unpunished violence and crime on the one hand, and fiscal oppression of small-business owners and police harassment of law-abiding drivers on the other.

In France, the vast majority of people feel like they have no control over the course of things. They witness the destiny of their country slipping away from them. They distrust their leaders but also their fellow citizens for being collectively responsible for this change.

The French people are more divided than ever. While a few decades ago people were divided based primarily on political grounds, the past few decades have led to the introduction of division, on new, legitimate grounds, based on religion, morals, ethnicity, contributions to society, and so on.

French society is now eminently divided and fragmented. Fewer and fewer people recognize in their fellow human being someone who shares sufferings, anxieties, and pains and as such who ought to be treated with politeness, kindness, and compassion. By default, others have become competitors, rivals, aggressors, invaders, traitors, fascists, idiots . . . Aggressiveness galore. Under these conditions, and in an amusing twist of events, it's actually become somewhat rebellious to be polite, thoughtful, and kind.

This perceived aggressiveness is only a symptom of the current state of France, which should prompt the French people to tackle the causes rather than the consequences of this phenomenon. Needless to say, there's some work to do—or, as the French say, *"C'est pas gagné!"*

Useful tip: Despite the frequent *agressivité*, bar fights are typically far less likely to erupt in France than in the U.S. or the UK.

Sound like a French person: *"Les gens sont à cran."* (People are on edge.)

GROCERY SHOPPING

❧

*G*rocery shopping in France can be as delightful as it can be disconcerting. When it comes to buying food on Gallic soil, your options fall within three main categories:

Le marché: Undoubtedly the most commonly spread image among Francophiles—the picture-perfect open-air market where beautiful local produce is on display, offering scents, textures, colors, and seasonal specialties straight out of an urban dweller's dream. Most towns, villages, or neighborhoods have their *jour du marché* frequented early in the morning by shoppers looking for the best quality and later in the day by those hoping for the best deal. In most parts of France, the local *marché* is a weekly invitation to fall in love with a place—and with a culture.

Le supermarché: French supermarkets offer certain strikingly disproportionate aisles. Strolling in the wine or cheese sections of a French supermarket will make you realize that certain clichés about France are still very much grounded in reality. It will also make you wonder how your local supermarket's cheapest wine option is this French supermarket's fanciest one. More surprising overly inflated sections include the yogurt and the *gâteaux* aisles. *Gâteaux* can be *sucrés* (cookies—which

French manufacturers take to a whole different level) or *salés* (savory, in which case they're dubbed *gâteaux apéro*).

France has a whole panoply of supermarkets, ranging from the huge *hypermarchés* (aka *les hyper*)—think Carrefour, E.Leclerc, Auchan—mostly on the outskirts of towns and cities; the *supermarchés* (aka *les grandes surfaces*)—Casino, Super U, etc.; all the way down to the charmingly named *supérettes*, which are somewhere between a local deli and a small supermarket. Some *supérettes* have more of an urban ring to them (Franprix, Monop'), while some have a more regional feel to them (Sherpa). Add to that grocery shopping topology what the French refer to as *le ardiscoont* (hard discount)—think Aldi, Lidl, Leader Price—and you'll have a good grasp of the love affair the French have developed with sizable chain retailers.

However, for shoppers familiar with the "nicer" retailers that have grown more popular in various places of the world over the past two decades, thanks to an average quality of products and shopping experience far superior to most of their competitors, such players have thus far failed to arise in France. French supermarkets do not offer the type of pleasurable grocery shopping experience the Whole Foods of the world have managed to develop. No matter how insanely prevalent it is in France, grocery shopping at a supermarket still has a vile undertone to it, one that somewhere in the backs of most French people's minds fosters a very discreet form of guilt stemming from the French suspicion (or knowledge) about what *la grande distribution* (large retailers) does in terms of exploitation of farmers, the triumph of large multinationals, and the destruction of the charm and independence of small local retailers. Aisle after aisle, French supermarkets offer a superb scene of utter oozing Frenchness: patrons pushing their carts with a very French air of mild reluctance and resignation, conveying to the world the sense that life—not just grocery shopping—is a chore. Add the exasperated looks in the checkout lane and the parents constantly scolding their children, and you'll have yourself a nice, incomparable French slice of Frenchness!

Les petits commerçants (also called *le commerce de proximité*): Think of the myriad *boulangeries* (bread), *fromageries* (cheese), *pâtisseries* (pastry), *boucheries* (meat), *charcuteries* (cured meats), *caves* (wine), *chocolateries* (chocolate), *fleuristes* (flowers), *traiteurs* (cooked dishes), *primeurs* (produce), *épiceries fines* (fine condiments)—most fully independent and fully artisanal—that make musing through French towns so enchanting and tempting. While the daily stop at the local boulangerie is still the norm for 90 percent of French people (mass-produced and freshly baked artisanal bread being worlds apart),[1] there is no doubt that all other artisans have suffered a great deal over the past decades as the French turned massively toward supermarkets for their convenience.

Consequently, while rarely as cheap as supermarkets, *les petits commerçants* that are still in business tend to offer stellar quality and a taste of a very lovable France, one that reminds us of a time when the independent shops of the *centre-villes* did not have to compete with ugly but more convenient and more easily accessible *zones commerciales* outside the city. *Les petits commerçants* are a weekend treat. Families go downtown on gourmet excursions on Saturday or Sunday mornings. Children marvel at the dead birds and chopped-off veals' heads at the butcher shop, pull their parents' pants at the bakery as they point to the bonbon section, pinch their noses *chez le fromager.* In this common family ritual lies a form of unspoken, vastly unconscious French form of education. The kids tag along and absorb the DNA of their country. Weekend after weekend, dead birds, pigs' brains, warm baguettes, and smelly cheeses become normal. Go figure: many grow up to become food snobs!

The king of the *commerce de bouche* is undoubtedly the boulangerie. Most French people are lucky enough to have several boulangeries to choose from. It shall be noted here that every single French household has a *boulangerie préférée*, which makes bread superior to the other ones in the vicinity and is absolutely worth the extra seconds or minutes

---

1 *"Les Français et le pain," TNS-Sofres,* March 21, 2005, www.tns-sofres.com/etudes-et-points-de-vue/les-francais-et-le-pain.

necessary to get to it. The level of intimacy most French people have with their local boulangerie(s) is such that they know what time of day warm bread and *viennoiseries* (croissants, pains au chocolat, etc.) come out of the oven or which boulangerie/pâtisserie near them makes the best *gâteaux* (cakes).

Next time you talk with a French person, please don't make a fool of yourself by naively implying that the local boulangerie making the best bread is the same one making the best pastries. Come on—you're better than this.

Useful tip: Go to *le marché*!

Sound like a French person: "*Moi non plus, j'aime pas faire mes courses dans un hyper, mais c'est plus pratique. Qu'est-ce que tu veux que je te dise? Je peux me garer. Je mets le petit dans le caddie . . .*" (I don't like to shop in huge supermarkets either, but it's more convenient. What can I say? It's easy to park. I can put the little one in the cart . . .)

NUTELLA

*F*rench cuisine is the subject of much passion, reverence, and sometimes controversy. Many foreigners imagine French kitchens to be wonderful treasure troves of mysterious spices wafting from sunlit pantries and homegrown herbs hanging from the ceiling.

However, the true secret weapon of a French kitchen is not rosemary, basil, or thyme.

It is Nutella.

The unsung trinity of French kitchens is as unlikely as it is a given: salt, pepper, Nutella. Nowhere else in the world has Nutella reached the status it has in France.

The Nutella culture in France is absolutely massive. Anyone in their thirties or younger grew up with Nutella. The ultimate versatile bribe for any parent—perfect on bread for breakfast or *goûter*—is undoubtedly the surest way to get a child to eat when he doesn't want to.

While the chocolaty hazelnut spread is generally found on bread, toast, croissants, or crêpes, any French person born after 1975 can remember the childhood delights of plunging a spoon into *un pot de Nutella* and sucking on the decadent spoonful. Bliss.

As one ages, the amount and frequency with which you eat Nutella usually drops. Nutella becomes an occasional treat, typically reserved for a special weekend or vacation breakfast.

The freshness of the *pot de Nutella*, revealed by its texture, is a clear indicator of just how much love the spread gets in the household. Storage conditions also have an impact on freshness and, just like ketchup, mustard, jam, or vinegar, Nutella is one of those household staples where two irreconcilable schools of thought coexist about the optimal way to store it: the fridge crowd vs. the cabinet posse. These two groups can, however, handle each other with only minor clashes between roommates or family members. That is not the case for the two sides of another, far more controversial argument over the beloved hazelnut spread.

This conflict involves those Nutella enthusiasts who refer to Nutella as feminine and those who refer to it as masculine: *le Nutella* vs. *la Nutella*. As masculine is the most commonly used, it will come as no surprise that any person using the feminine will be viewed as a weirdo.

One generation ago, when Nutella initially gained popularity, most parents bought Nutella to satisfy their children, but very few consumed it. Attempts to suggest noble substitutes like honey or jam were frequent but typically pointless. The expression *cochonnerie* was commonly applied. Usually counterproductively, since what grown-ups call *cochonneries*, ranging from bonbons to Nutella, from chewing gum to marshmallows . . . is obviously the good stuff.

One generation later, the Nutella kids are now Nutella parents. And the splurging no longer divides French families. Finally, French parents absolutely understand that Nutella is delicious and it's no longer uncommon to walk into a kitchen and catch Mom or Dad savoring a spoonful straight from the jar.

Useful tip: It's really bad for you, but if you've never done it before, make sure to eat a full spoonful of Nutella at least once.

Sound like a French person: *"Il reste du Nut?"* (Any Nutella left?)

PATRIOTIC BRAVADO

❦

When interacting with foreigners, many French people make it very clear that France has the best stuff in the world.

Food? French is the best.

Style? Nothing beats French fashion.

Wine? Seriously, you want to go there?

The logic extends beyond the areas for which France is traditionally well-known worldwide. Anytime a song composed by a French artist gets played overseas, the French person in attendance will not physically be able to hold back from saying smugly, "Did you know they're French?"

This statement will bring utmost satisfaction when the words of the song are in English (like most David Guetta, Daft Punk, and electro French songs). Bliss.

While they fool (and frequently aggravate) most non-French, these statements could come as a surprise to anyone who happens to know France from the inside. For within the reality of our global marketplace, the average French person has primarily become a pizza eater who buys his clothes from H&M, drinks Coke, and listens to Rihanna.

While they still specialize in occasional grandiloquent pro-French-stuff statements overseas, most French people know deep down that what they're doing is truly putting on a show.

The reality they witness on a daily basis exemplifies the exact opposite of their occasional patriotic bravado. Most French people are extremely aware of the dilapidation of the French cultural heritage. The proclaimed supremacy of the French stuff they champion overseas has more to do with a symbolic joust in favor of what they wish their country still was, rather than with a deep conviction that France is home to the best things in the world.

The French, like most mildly annoying people, are just a little broken inside.

Useful tip: Give French people a hug and tell them they'll be okay.

Sound like a French person: *"Pour tout ce qui est train, on est quand même les meilleurs du monde."* (For anything train-related, we're the best in the world.)

THE FRENCH-
AMERICAN DREAM

$\mathbb{S}$ ome say the American dream is dead. Not in France.

While the odds of someone from a very humble background making it big are quite slim in France, some have recently showed that it is an actual possibility. *Le rags* to *le riches*!

While real financial poverty in France is typically rural poverty in places where jobs and physical access to opportunities are scarce,[1] the collective perception is that real poverty lies in the *banlieues*—the outskirts of larger cities.

French *banlieues* have grown to develop a culture of their own, with their own language, their own myths, their own heroes. Some of these heroes are people who grew up in the *banlieues*, were shaped by their roughness, and yet managed to make it big. The most common examples are to be found in three fields:

- **Sports:** The following names might not resonate with American readers who are not versed in soccer, but the French *banlieues*

---

1 Cécile Crouzel, *"Les banlieues sont moins pauvres que certaines villes et zones rurales,"* Le Figaro, June 2, 2015, www.lefigaro.fr/conjoncture/2015/06/02/20002-20150602ARTFIG00006-les-banlieues -sont-moins-pauvres-que-certaines-villes-et-zones-rurales.php.

have honed countless professional players, as well as some of the greatest talents in the game over the past two decades: Nicolas Anelka, Karim Benzema, the list goes on. In these players' attitude remains an indefectible *banlieue* touch in the form of a roughness, an angularity that fame, success, and riches have not managed to brush off. These traits are a double-edged sword. Once success is there, these guys are typically considered larger than life to those in their poor neighborhoods who can recognize and appreciate the firm steadiness that tends to characterize these players. Fans who don't understand what they have gone through struggle to connect with the absence of smiles, the way of speaking, and the unpolished air of these multimillionaire boys.

- **Rap:** Rap emanates from the *banlieues* and its most illustrious names are pure *banlieusards*: *des mecs des quartiers* (guys from the hood). While the money and fame can't compare with that of soccer stars, there is no doubt that big rappers—big names like Booba, La Fouine, Rohff, etc.—have manifested a form of success and a sense of accomplishment and recognition that many aspire to.

- **Comedy:** In the wake of the success of comedian Jamel Debbouze, a generation of comedians from the *banlieues* has grown to be big in the world of comedy and entertainment. The most striking example is probably Omar Sy, who recently appeared in Hollywood blockbusters like *X-Men: Days of Future Past* and *Jurassic World*.

Just like in impoverished urban areas in America, many in the French *banlieues* dream of success in rap or sports. Just like in America, some make it. There too, however, the odds are slim. Probably more so than in America, many youngsters feel that other opportunities—those requiring an education—are simply too far for them to reach. This new French dream, shared by countless teenagers, surely reflects the Americanization of the culture and aspirations in growing sections of the French territory and population. It is, however, a much-needed dream, one that some have realized, and one that generates treasures of hope, pride, energy, and motivation.

Ultimately, it does not matter if not many squeeze through the tiny exit door. The French *banlieue* has its heroes and its role models. Associating hard work and tremendous rewards in the minds of millions of young French people will no doubt reap tremendous rewards for the country in the decades to come, far beyond the world of sports and rap. Watch it, world: French youth is only getting stronger!

Useful tip: Check out the video *94, c'est le Barça* (the number 94 is a *banlieue* zip code and Barça is one of the most prestigious and successful soccer teams in the world).

Sound like a French person: *"Et l'autre là, ça lui écorcherait la face, un sourire?"* (Look at that one—would a smile hurt his face?)

IDEOLOGICAL
TRANSFORMATIONS

The cultural paradigm at work in France is that of a certain cultural liberalism: on paper, all members of French society can live their lives freely as they intend it.

While this sounds ideal in theory, it has led to what the French call *les problèmes de société*, causing rifts to form between different groups of people. Examples are daily and countless: advocates work toward gay marriage, which divides them and their supporters from religious Muslims and Christians who hold opposite beliefs; those pushing for more government spending against those who want lower taxes; even activists combating GMO farming, who frustrate agro-science professionals. The direct consequence of these divides is an increased atomization of French society, which pushes people to turn inward toward their own communities—others with the same views and belief systems— to find mental and spiritual refuge.

The proportion of French people who share common values is shrinking at a fast pace. However, there is one thing most humans have in common: money. The market reunites for a few moments people who are otherwise different in every possible way. In every French city, Saturday is the day of *le shopping*, and entire crowds, of all colors, origins, and creeds, flock to the new temples of modern consumption. Their common identity stems from consumption. The new normal—in France like in so many other countries—is a slow but constant morphing of unique individuals into a vague bunch of apathetic but sovereign consumers.

As an example, the sense of the importance of beauty is no longer as commonly shared in France as Francophiles would think. You can hate the hideous *zones commerciales* that have popped up all over the French territory, disfiguring the landscape, but there is little to be done about that. In this new society, aesthetic sensibilities are by essence personal and consequently irrelevant to overriding political action and financial gain. The result of this approach is that, short of a common moral, aesthetic, or philosophical compass uniting people, all issues are resolved based solely on how the economy will be impacted. In a very un-French twist, the new religion of economic growth is to substitute itself for the absence of common morality and philosophy.

Until recently, it was a peculiar charm of the French that not everything boiled down to money, the economy, and the market. The French mind-set tended to value things like conviviality or beauty over money and profit. But at some point the legal, ideological, and fiscal framework of the country pointed the compass in a new direction, somewhere east of mercantile and north of consumerism.

As a consequence, the French might have lost some charm and their country grown less pretty, but that is inevitably put into perspective of the true valuable measure of success in a modern society: economic growth. Surely, money is spent and money is earned. The cult of endless economic growth on a finite planet, in a country where growth has been dwindling for several years, is still going strong.

Nevertheless, terms like *sobriété heureuse* (happy sobriety) and *décroissance volontaire* (voluntary decline) are popping up in conversations more and more frequently in certain circles. It is a beautiful thing to see people going against their programming in a country where the entirety of the political class repeats incessantly that the key to a successful society is more growth, more productivity, more purchasing power, and—ultimately—more consumption.

Useful tip: Research shows that spending money on experiences rather than things is more conducive to happiness.

Sound like a French person: *"Mais tu ne peux plus dire des choses comme ça de nos jours!"* (But you just can't say things like that anymore these days!)

THE OBSESSION
WITH FOOD

∞

*F*ood has long been a French obsession. As such, the vocabulary of food has deeply penetrated the French language.

The extent of it is unfathomable to most non-Francophones. So while a French person who learns a few food terms in English can then order food in English, the foreigner who learns a few French food terms can travel throughout the French-speaking world and get to experience nothing less than the full range of life's events and emotions.

Life hack: To become fluent in French, just focus on food terms.

Okay, let's start easy:

This girl's ugly!
C'est un thon! (She's a tuna!)

But that guy still wants to have sex!
Mais il veut tremper le biscuit! (He wants to dip the biscuit!)

Turns out she's gonna get some!
Elle va passer à la casserole! (She's getting in the saucepan!)

He's put on quite a belly!
Il a pris de la brioche! (He's taken on some brioche!)

Does he have a good job?

Il a un bon gagne-pain? (Does he have a good breadwinner?)

Mind your own business!

Occupe-toi de tes oignons! (Mind your onions!)

We got into an argument.

On s'est frités. (We French-fried each other).

He lied to me!

Il m'a raconté des salades! (He told me salads!)

He started to make a big deal out of it.

Il en a fait tout un fromage. (He made a cheese out of it).

So I punched him and knocked him out.

Donc je lui ai mis une patate et il est tombé dans les pommes. (So I gave him a potato and he fell in the apples.)

Did you see that fat guy?

Tu as vu le gros lard? (Did you see the big lard?)

With the tall girl?

Avec la grande asperge? (With the big asparagus?)

He lives three blocks from here.

Il habite à trois pâtés de maisons. (He lives three house pâtés from here.)

Speed up!

Appuie sur le champignon! (Press on the mushroom!)

We're gonna get soaked!

On va se faire saucer! (We're gonna get sauced!)

You're annoying.
T'es casse-bonbons. (You're a candy breaker.)
C'est un navet, ce film, de toute façon! (This movie is a turnip anyway!)

Now, some foods terms the French simply love . . . a little too much. *Chou* is one of them. *Chou* means "cabbage"; in the world of pastry—and in most of the following phrases—it also refers to a delicious and adorable little puff. In France, you can have entire conversations using only that one word:

He's so cute!
Il est chou! (He's cabbage!)

Yes, but he's getting on my nerves!
Oui, mais il me broute le chou! (He's grazing my cabbage!) Or, alternately: *Il me court sur le haricot!* (He's running on my bean!)

He's only a kid!
Mais c'est un p'tit bout de chou! (He's a little piece of cabbage!)

Don't worry about it!
Te prends pas le chou avec ça! (Don't take your cabbage with that!)

I know. I'm out of it.
Je sais. J'suis dans les choux. (I'm in the cabbages.)

Another such word is *patate*, which is the colloquial form of *pomme de terre* (potato, or literally "apple of the earth"):

I'm all shaken up!
J'en ai gros sur la patate! (I have a lot on my potato!)

The guy was punching everyone.

Il distribuait des patates. (He was distributing potatoes.)

It's going to cost him a hundred grand.

Ça va lui coûter cent patates. (It's going to cost him a hundred potatoes.)

That guy's such an idiot!

Mais quelle patate, ce mec! (That guy's such a potato!)

Boudin (blood sausage) is another French favorite:

Are you pouting?

Tu fais du boudin? (Are you making blood sausage?)

No, but she's so ugly!

Non, mais quel boudin! (What a blood sausage!)

In France, like in any other country, you have to deal with your fair share of stupid people. Generously, the French language offers a lovely display of food items to deal lightheartedly with such unfortunate characters. The following food items all refer to an idiot, but each with a different nuance, a certain level of endearment, and a specific target group:

Someone's really bad at what they do?

That's *une truffe* (a truffle) or *une crêpe* (a crêpe)!

A woman does not exactly display brilliance?

She's *une courge* (a squash).

Need to gently call someone out for a silly move? Call them *une nouille* (a noodle), *un cornichon* (a gherkin), *une patate* (a potato), *une pomme* (an apple), *une andouille* (sausage generally made from pork intestines), or *une banane* (a banana). Those are quite endearing terms, frequently used to kindly mock children when they do something silly. Later on in life, wives will start using them on their husbands.

That is, if the relationship is a good one. If the relationship turns sour (*si les choses tournent au vinaigre*—if things turn to vinegar), or if the husband starts losing it (*s'il pédale dans la choucroute*—if he pedals in sauerkraut), food terms simply won't cut it.

If that happens, even though they might get upset (*la moutarde leur monte au nez*—mustard goes up their nose), both halves of the couple will have to stay upbeat (*garder la pêche* or *garder la frite*—keep the peach or keep the French fry), and smile (*avoir la banane*—have the banana).

It is not easy (*ce n'est pas de la tarte*—it's not pie), as one of them might be drunk too often (*être beurré*—be buttered), be ungrateful (*cracher dans la soupe*—spit in the soup), or simply have thin skin (*être soupe au lait*—be milk soup). It is key to toning it down (*mettre de l'eau dans son vin*—put water in your wine) and not to tell the other to get lost (*d'aller se faire cuire un oeuf*—to go cook himself an egg).

For if they don't, it might end up costing them a lot (*l'addition peut être salée*—the check can be salty) and they would have to spend a lot of money (*beaucoup d'oseille*—a lot of sorrel), sometimes leaving one of them penniless (*sans un radis*—without a radish). At that point, it's game over (*les carottes sont cuites*—the carrots are cooked)! Soon enough, they'll both end up with graying hair (*poivre et sel*—salt and pepper) and with the feeling of having been owned (*de s'être fait carotter*—having been "carroted"). Next thing you know, they start going senile (*ils commencent à sucrer les fraises*—they start to sprinkle sugar on the strawberries), and if it's the real deal (*si c'est pas du flan*—if it's not flan), then let me tell you: it is not an easy situation (*c'est pas du gâteau*—it's not cake)!

Useful tip: The teacher's pet in France is referred to as *le chouchou*.

Sound like a French person: *"Allez, on a du pain sur la planche!"* (Come on, we've got some work to do! [Literally: We've got bread on the board!])

PERMISSIVENESS

Some stories would legitimately be rejected by movie producers for not being realistic enough.

So it's the story of a convicted pedophile who's reinstated as a schoolteacher and who goes back to abusing more pupils.

Nah . . . not really believable!

All right, fair enough. How about this one: a school principal who gets stabbed by a parent who's already been busted several times for trying to kill people.

Come on, get real now.

All right, now I have a good one: in Paris, this girl gets killed after being stabbed in the face with a screwdriver by a guy who has already been arrested thirty-seven times for all sorts of crimes.

Unfortunately, the three scenarios above are true stories.[1] They— along with thousands of others in the same vein—all happened recently

---

1 *"Paris: Une directrice d'école poignardée, l'agresseur interpellé," Le Parisien,* February 19, 2015, http://leparisien.fr/paris-75/paris-une-directrice-d-ecole-poignardee-19-02-2015-4546899.php.

in France. Because in France, if you break the law—should you happen to get caught—most likely your sentence will be more of a vague slap on the wrist than an actual deterring sanction.

Commit a petty crime in France and chances are the only thing you're in for is a good talking to. Feel like sexually assaulting a child? Fair enough. On average, if you get caught, you'll spend fifteen months in prison.[2] Now you're feeling cheeky and you want to murder someone. You incorrigible you! Well, knock yourself out! Worse comes to worst: your average prison time for murdering someone in France is 6.2 years.[3]

The general permissiveness of the French judicial system has several clear consequences:

- A legitimate feeling of impunity for most criminals.
- A legitimate feeling of exasperation for most law-abiding citizens.
- A general sense of the whole system being a disturbingly sick joke.

Commit a crime and you'll find a battalion of *gauchiste* souls to find you a million excuses. For them, the real culprits for your crime are well identified: poverty, violence, despair, drugs, education—you name it. Anything but good old individual responsibility (these last two words being nowhere to be found in a French *gauchiste* dictionary). You, my friend, have very little to do with murdering that person. You, my friend, are the real victim here.

Several decades of slow amplification of this nonsense have given way not only to tragedies by the thousands but also to a complete degradation of the French social fabric.

"*Isère: émoi après l'arrestation d'un instit déjà condamné pour pédopornographie,*" *Le Parisien,* March 24, 2015, www.leparisien.fr/faits-divers/isere-l-interpellation-d-un-directeur-d-ecole-soupconne-de-viols-cree-l-emoi-24-03-2015-4632471.php.

"*La jeune femme agressée à coups de tournevis à Paris est morte,*" *Le Figaro,* December 26, 2014, www.lefigaro.fr/actualite-france/2014/12/26/01016-20141226ARTFIG00154-la-jeune-femme-agressee-a-coups-de-tournevis-a-paris-est-morte.php.

2 Naja, "*Statistiques de la police et de la justice sur les violences sexuelles en France,*" *Agora Vox,* May 4, 2009, http://mobile.agoravox.fr/actualites/societe/article/statistiques-de-la-police-et-de-la-55516.

3 "*09 B VIII. La longueur des peines en France,*" *Ban Public,* April 6, 2007, http://prison.eu.org/spip.php?article9272.

The French left having championed this *culture de l'excuse*, it is with mild delight that the cheeky right-wing Frenchie will observe French leftists—young and old—being mugged and beaten up with a sadly routine frequency at the end of public events in France. Think fireworks, Bastille Day celebrations, big game nights, or public concerts are typically joyful and peaceful events in France? Think again. In 2013, when the Paris soccer team, Paris Saint-Germain (PSG), won the French championship, *racailles* (hoodlums) took to the streets of the Trocadéro area of Paris for several hours and pretty much looted, mugged, and destroyed anything they could find.

La culture de l'excuse gives way to *la culture de l'impunité*. French leftists and French hoodlums together have managed to deteriorate the quality of life in France. Anything fully open to the public is now always slightly ominous due to the threat of a fight breaking out or the destruction of property. French authorities are starting to realize it: during the last soccer World Cup, the city of Paris chose not to set up a giant screen for Parisians and tourists to enjoy the games in a cheerful atmosphere. At public events, the French struggle to be cheerful these days, and more and more people avoid them for fear of a few ruining the event for the many.

Fun times!!

Useful tip: Watch your pockets and handbags in the Parisian metro.

Sound like a French person: *"Ah ça, pour emmerder les gens normaux, y a du monde . . ."* (Harassing law-abiding citizens—that they're good at!)

BREAKFAST
AND COFFEE

*I*n many countries, breakfast is viewed as a real meal. At home, proper warm food is prepared, cooking pans are used, etc. People regularly meet up for breakfast: diners, restaurants, and cafés offer a proper breakfast menu and patrons show up to eat it. Sure, people usually just grab something like cereal or toast on your typical weekday, but "breakfast food" is a real category of food that most people can identify immediately (and that some people occasionally have for lunch or dinner).

When it comes to its breakfast culture, France is a completely different ball game. No warm food, no eggs, no sausage, no bacon. Not even on the weekends. Your typical French *petit-déjeuner* consists of bread with some sort of spread or topping, called *tartines*. Consumed for breakfast by 75 percent of French people, typically *tartines* are spread with butter, jam, honey, or Nutella, with a strong cup of coffee alongside. Other common staples include cereal with milk, fruit juice, fresh fruit, yogurt, or *viennoiseries* such as a croissant or pain au chocolat.

Incidentally, while an overwhelming majority of French people know full well that breakfast is an essential meal, almost a fifth of them frequently just skip it.[1] Not only is your typical French breakfast poor in terms of nutrition, it is also by far the most underwhelming one of the day in terms of appeal. While bread and croissants are typically delicious in France—that is, *fresh* bread and croissants—few people are running out to the boulangerie before breakfast every morning, especially on weekends. Most therefore settle for bread from the day before or mass-produced supermarket bread, resulting in morning meals that are not exactly haute cuisine. Consequently, most French people approach breakfast with very little excitement. Restaurants don't offer a breakfast menu, and suggesting to meet a friend or client for breakfast would be considered very odd in France.

The poor nutritional value of the French *petit-déjeuner* might explain why the French are such ravenous coffee drinkers. Fully 90 percent of the French drink coffee and 85 percent do so every day. It is striking to note that the French drink coffee far more routinely than they do wine, all stereotypes to the contrary.[2] And overall, espresso is king as far as types of coffee consumed. Coffee is typically served with breakfast, after lunch, and commonly during the many *pauses café*, or coffee breaks, French workers like to take. One of the surprising characteristics for someone visiting France is the number of vending machines that sell coffee. They're everywhere—at the office, in gas stations, in metro stations, on the streets, in train stations—and some make a hot brew that's not as bad as you might think. Add to this the countless cafés found throughout the country and you can rest assured: getting your coffee fix on French soil will *never* be a problem.

1 Keren Lentschner, *"Le petit-déjeuner n'a plus la cote en France,"* Le Figaro, October 1, 2014, www.lefigaro.fr/societes/2014/10/01/20005-20141001ARTFIG00075-le-petit-dejeuner-n-a-plus-la-cote-en-france.php.

2 Christelle Granja, *"Modes de vie: les Européens accros au café,"* My Europ, July 22, 2014, http://fr.myeurop.info/2014/07/22/modes-de-vie-europeens-accros-cafe-12659.

Useful tip: French bakeries typically open quite early. There is a lot of joy to derive from patronizing a bakery at six a.m. Either after a great party or at the start of a long day!

Sound like a French person: *"Café? Quatre cafés, s'il vous plaît!"* (Coffee? Four coffees, please!)

LA QUENELLE

Traditionally, a *quenelle* is a somewhat heavy—yet delicious—ball of pounded fish or meat. It's a rugby-ball-shaped food specialty from Lyon. Lately, however, pronouncing the word *quenelle* in France will spark controversy.

Not because rich food has suddenly become suspicious in France, but because the word *quenelle* no longer refers to just a pastry. The word's new accepted definition has become the foundation of a new cultural, legal, and political controversy. Controversy based on food terminology: welcome to France!

For millions of Frenchies, *glisser une quenelle* (literally, "shoving a quenelle") has become an irreverent quirky gesture. The gesture itself, *une quenelle*, is simple: place one hand over your opposite shoulder, and extend the arm below that shoulder. Perfect execution comes from the command of the movement of sliding/shoving.

Both the gesture and the terms were introduced over a decade ago by French comedian Dieudonné, who used it repeatedly, year after year, in his skits as one of his signature comedic gimmicks.

Mention *la quenelle* in France and most will immediately associate the term with Dieudonné. He is an unusual character. He rose to fame as part of the most popular comedic duo of the nineties (Élie et

Dieudonné). After a while, the two split up and pursued solo careers. Dieudonné's career tanked brutally in 2003 after a (relatively unfunny) skit on live TV where he mocked an Israeli settler. Shortly after, the media notified him and the general French public that he had crossed a line. Unexpectedly enough, Dieudonné chose not to repent or apologize.

His career nose-dived. He ceased to be invited on TV shows and got publicly demonized and vilified in the press. Some of his rants got more radical: his vocal criticisms of Israel, Zionism, and the Jewish lobby rank between suspicious and unacceptable to a large chunk of the French population, who in turn see Dieudonné as *un antisémite*—no redemption possible.[1]

To another fraction of the French population, however, Dieudonné's positions are viewed as a beacon of genuine freedom of speech in a country that has mostly lost the courage or the will to exercise it. In this category, some say, *"Il dit la vérité"* (He speaks the truth); others simply argue, *"On s'en fiche, tant qu'il est drôle?"* (Who cares, as long as he's funny?).

Over the past few years, Dieudonné has grown to become a very polarizing figure. Some hate him; some love him. Some argue that he's no longer a comedian; others obviously disagree, as his shows are typically jam-packed, making him undoubtedly one of France's most popular comedians.[2]

His detractors fight him tooth and nail, from the French prime minister publicly denouncing him over[3] and over again to a well-known journalist announcing that Dieudonné's being executed would fill him

---

1 Ouri Wesoly, *"Pour ceux qui croient encore que Dieudonné n'est pas antisémite,"* CCLJ, January 2, 2014, www.cclj.be/actu/politique-societe/pour-ceux-qui-croient-encore-que-dieudonne-est-pas-antisemite.

2 *"Dieudonné meilleures ventes à la FNAC, comme tous les ans,"* Media Libre, July 20, 2012, www.medialibre.eu/breves/dieudonne-meilleures-ventes-a-la-fnac-comme-tous-les-ans/12557.

3 *"Manuel Valls charge Dieudonné devant l'Assemblée nationale,"* Sud Ouest, January 13, 2015, www.sudouest.fr/2015/01/13/manuel-valls-charge-dieudonne-devant-l-assemblee-nationale-1795641-6092.php.

with joy,[4] from countless lawsuits[5] to tax audits[6] and more. The harassment strategy at play might be questionable, as it tends to make a case in favor of Dieudonné's vocal antiestablishment message (i.e., against mainstream media and politicians, all presented as sellouts). However (or consequently), Dieudonné remains prolific on- and off-line. His influence makes his messages gain momentum among a certain French population, while another France considers the whole ordeal with a mix of contempt, fear, and suspicion.

Dieudonné's "us versus them" rhetoric, presenting the French people as oppressed by the powers that be, made *la quenelle* spread like wildfire. It was the *signe de ralliement*, the cheeky "up yours" against the ruling class.

People started taking quirky *quenelle* pictures with politicians. Mockery and irreverence spread. Police officers, military personnel, nurses, teachers, athletes, correctional officers—everyone was having fun taking *photos quenelles*.

The crackdown was swift.

La quenelle entered a new phase as mainstream media started to depict it as an anti-Semitic gesture. As the gesture was initiated by Dieudonné, who is critical of Zionism, painting everyone who does a *quenelle* as an anti-Semite seemed fair to some. A French Jewish lobby stated boldly that the *quenelle* gesture symbolized sodomizing the victims of the Holocaust. Bit too much? Nah! Overnight, anybody doing a *quenelle* had officially become an *antisémite*.

And then there was the crackdown. The government gave orders and several government employees lost their jobs. A twenty-three-year-old electrician got fined[7] for a *photo quenelle* with the prime minister.

---

4 Philippe Tesson on Radio Classique, accessible at www.youtube.com/watch?v=Q4eBu7OPdSw.

5 *"Dieudonné perd-il tous ses procès?,"* *Metro News*, April 14, 2016, www.metronews.fr/info/dieudonne-perd-il-tous-ses-proces-videos/mpbx!Hi4BLkkoQgc8/.

6 *"Contrôle fiscal à la société de production des spectacles de Dieudonné,"* *JDD*, February 5, 2014, www.lejdd.fr/Societe/Justice/Controle-fiscal-a-la-societe-de-production-des-spectacles-de-Dieudonne-651705.

7 *"Lyon: Condamné à 500 euros d'amende pour avoir fait une 'quenelle' à Manuel Valls,"* *20 Minutes*, March 15, 2016, www.20minutes.fr/lyon/1806783-20160315-isere-500-euros-amende-avoir-fait-quenelle-manuel-valls.

Military personnel were discharged[8] from the French military; high schoolers were suspended[9] from school for a week. One soccer star who celebrated a goal with a *quenelle* had to leave his club.[10] A few weeks after the start of the crackdown phase, most people stopped doing *quenelles*. Somehow, the risk of losing one's job, paired with the threat of being suspected for life of being an anti-Semite, ceased to be worth the fun photo op.

Useful tip: If you understand French, check out funny Frenchmen Julien Cazarre or Augustin Shackelpopoulos.

Sound like a French person: "*Dieudonné . . . oulah, il est complètement antisémite, lui!*" (Dieudonné, he's a total anti-Semite, that one!)

8 "*Lille: Cinq gradés contestent leur sanction pour une quenelle,*" *20 Minutes*, January 6, 2016, www.20minutes.fr/lille/1760527-20160106-lille-cinq-grades-contestent-sanction-quenelle.
9 "*Charente-Maritime: La quenelle indigeste de cinq lycéens,*" *Sud Ouest*, November 5, 2015, www.sudouest.fr/2015/11/05/charente-maritime-la-quenelle-indigeste-de-cinq-lyceens-2175724-1391.php.
10 "*Affaire de la 'quenelle': Anelka résilie son contrat avec West Bromwich,*" *Le Point*, March 14, 2014, www.lepoint.fr/sport/affaire-de-la-quenelle-anelka-resilie-son-contrat-avec-west-bromwich-14-03-2014-1801303_26.php.

LES ANGLO-SAXONS

$\mathcal{F}$rench people, there is no doubt about it, are comfortable with abstractions.

One of the most essential abstract concepts any foreigner visiting France should grow more accustomed to is that of the *Anglo-Saxon*.

In the French psyche, *les Anglo-Saxons* are a species in their own right, a wonderfully compact mass of humans, sharing a language and other qualities. While the core of the notion refers to Great Britain and the United States, French people won't be shy about adding Canada, Australia, and New Zealand to the group. Now, some givens ought to be understood before one engages in a discussion with a French person. They go as follows:

Who's always drinking? *Les Anglo-Saxons.*
Which people is always warmongering? *Les Anglo-Saxons.*
Who's undermining the French language? *Les Anglo-Saxons.*
Who's really good at business? *Les Anglo-Saxons.*
Whose mentality is centered on money? *Les Anglo-Saxons.*
Who's got really good universities and research? *Les Anglo-Saxons.*

Those six premises will help any foreigner converse constructively with French people. Should you originate from an *"Anglo-Saxon"* nation yourself and therefore be prone to rejecting such simplistic views, be warned: any attempt to do so will lead you to being perceived as the arrogant, dominating, imperialistic prick your sorry Anglo-Saxon self truly is.

The fact that the English mentality might somehow differ from the American mentality is enough of a stretch. If such an argument is brought to the table, the French person typically shifts the blame discussion to one given country. Let's face it—that means the United States.

It is well-known among the French that the United States is not a diverse country. A liberal from the Bay Area thinks exactly like a Mormon from Salt Lake City, and a first-generation Honduran immigrant in Houston shares the same worldview as an old-money billionaire in Connecticut.

Les Anglo-Saxons are one united bunch, and ultimately they're out to get some French you-know-what. It is key to realize that pulling out the old *Anglo-Saxon* card will not make the speaker sound like a conspiracy theorist. *Au contraire*: those who gripe about *Anglo-Saxons* pass for insightful observers of the world and of the forces that shape it. The French press specializes in the skillful drop of *Anglo-Saxon* bombs. There is no doubt that using a complex-sounding term to refer to a nonexistent force outside of France in order to prove a point is textbook French journalism. But as the French put it, no matter how bad the French press is, it's far better than . . . *la presse anglo-saxonne*!

Useful tip: Best way to dodge the Anglo-Saxon objectification: when asked where you're from, prefer a city/region/state.

Sound like a French person: *"Mais ça, c'est la culture anglo-saxonne—typique!"* (That's textbook Anglo-Saxon culture for you!)

MASSES AND
MOSQUES

⌘

Since the inception of Vatican II, France went from being *la fille aînée de l'église* (the first child of the Catholic Church) to being one of the least religious countries on earth. Among the general public, the Church went from being viewed as a profoundly respected and heeded institution to being an inaudible and questionable organization.

Over the past decades, institutional antireligiosity has characterized France. The Church and Christianity have been incessantly mocked and ridiculed. Believers were portrayed as gullible fools and clerics as pedophiles. *Les Cathos* remain in existence but are viewed more and more by the rest of the country as a backward, vaguely suspect group. Catholics in France are now viewed as being on the margins of society.

The subject of religion has vastly disappeared from the conversations of the French middle class. The bourgeoisie will occasionally indulge in discourses reflecting a very loose and malleable interpretation of religious dogma, picking what they fancy as if religion were a spiritual buffet. The shift is not only spiritual; it is also physical. In France, every year several churches—frequently old and beautiful ones—get demolished (typically under the pretense that maintenance is too expensive).[1] No matter how empty they are, the symbolic brutality of the destruction of those beautiful churches is devastating.

However, it would be mistaken to consider France as a country where religion is dying out. For while churches are being torn apart, mosques are being built at a steady pace: over the past decade, every week an average of one to two new mosques opened their doors in France.[2] While in 1976 there were only 150 mosques in France, there are now more than 2,200, with several hundred—some grandiose—being built as you read this text. In many areas of France, *boucheries halal* (halal butcheries) have become the only option for buying fresh meat. Heck, the meals served to the French national soccer team at the 2010 World Cup were halal. Witnessing a doubling of their sales when offering a halal menu, fast-food chain Quick decided to make a number of its restaurants halal-only.[3] While virtually inexistent thirty years ago, more than ten thousand kebab restaurants now sprinkle the French territory. Those complaining about the Americanization of France will be happy to learn that there are at least seven times more kebab joints than McDonald's on French soil.

The tremendous surge of Islam is a response to the collapse of the Catholic Church.

Because Islam offers a sense of right and wrong and connects a certain French youth to an active and growing cause and community, it has gained tremendous ground in France recently. While official reports continue to claim that Catholicism is still the number one religion in France—which happens to be impossible to prove since the French state is prohibited from keeping such statistics—there is no doubt that if it is still the case (which is unlikely), it won't be for long.

---

1 *"La destruction des églises de France,"* *Reinformation*, April 21, 2015, http://reinformation.tv/destruction-eglises-france/.

2 Laurent Dandrieu, *"Mosquées en France, l'inquiétante invasion,"* *Valeurs Actuelles*, May 15, 2014, www.valeursactuelles.com/societe/mosquees-en-france-linquietante-invasion-45541.

3 "Popular French Fast Food Chain Causes Controversy by Introducing Halal-Only Food," *Daily Mail*, September 2, 2010, www.dailymail.co.uk/news/article-1308366/Popular-French-fast-food-chain-Quick-causes-controversy-introducing-halal-food.html.

In France, only 16 percent of practicing Catholics are under thirty-four years old, as opposed to 46 percent of Muslims.[4]

While most French people have entirely turned their backs on their Christian heritage and many openly mock Christianity and Christians, very few apply the same rhetoric to Islam. When it comes to the spread of Islam, the French people bold enough to vocalize their concern usually go to painstaking lengths to be sure everyone knows that "they respect Islam and Muslim people" and that "Islam is a religion of peace" or that "faith is a wonderful thing." Needless to say, they do not go through such trouble before bashing Christianity. Nothing says strong people like double standards, and deference to mask fear.

Useful tip: In order to sound like you know what you're doing in a kebab joint, just mention *salade, tomates, oignons* as if it were entirely obvious. Extra points if you add *sauce samouraï*!

Sound like a French person: *"Mais ça a rien à voir avec l'Islam, ça. Et les Croisades?!"* (This has nothing to do with Islam! And what about the Crusades, then?!)

4 Jean-Marie Guénois, *"L'Islam, première religion en France?," Le Figaro*, October 25, 2012, www .lefigaro.fr/actualite-france/2012/10/24/01016-20121024ARTFIG00633-islam-premiere -religion-en-france.php.

LA MONDIALISATION

$\mathcal{F}$rench people love to debate grandiose notions and vague concepts. *La mondialisation* (globalization) is clearly no exception.

Should you be imprudent enough to engage in such a conversation with French people, make sure to get your sword out—things are about to get heated.

The natural inclination of most French people is to see any new phenomenon, particularly if it has to do with the economy, as a threat. Engulfed in their negativity, very few French people are able to see opportunities in the changing times. Consequently, 78 percent of French people have a negative opinion of globalization.[1] This staggering number undoubtedly highlights the deep defiance many French people have developed toward the capitalist model.

When hearing the term *mondialisation*, the French mind gets overwhelmed with images of factories being closed down, sensations of the French language disappearing, mild fears of terrible pollution, and contaminated food flooding the market. Very few think about affordable

---

1 *"78% des Français ont une image négative de la mondialisation,"* Le Monde, April 11, 2012, www.le monde.fr/economie/article/2012/04/11/78-des-francais-ont-une-image-negative-de -la-mondialisation_1684024_3234.html.

cell phones, flat-screen TVs, more efficiency in their jobs, cheap vacations, and many other conveniences of modern life that the French are as quick to enjoy as anyone else.

The French struggle to reconcile the fact that they want the latest iPhone at a low price but that they're not happy when factories shut down in France. They feel that more openness means that ultimately they will get the worst end of the deal. The French have indoctrinated themselves into thinking that change typically results in being worse off. Their ability to adapt collectively is suffering. All the more so as the country is chasing off its talent at an alarming pace. In this new context, France's ability to create new jobs and new industries has proven to be rather disappointing.

In France, the concern over the topic of globalization holds less true among the younger generation who was born into it. They learned, to their detriment, that the post–World War II *modèle social* that previous generations were so keen to defend and preserve had nothing good or realistic to offer them. Faced with very high unemployment rates, most younger French people are struggling to find relevance or interest in pursuing a collective—and even less so national—destiny. The idea of saving French culture from globalization doesn't occur to them—their culture and their world are already global.

Useful tip: Look into the work of Pierre Rabhi.

Sound like a French person: *"Mais le modèle de la mondialisation hyper libérale, c'est horrible."* (But the model of ultracapitalist globalization is a terrible thing.)

FRENCH CINEMA

𝔗he French have had a long love story with cinema. From the Lu-
mière brothers, who invented it, to Max Linder—whom Charlie
Chaplin viewed as his master—to the rise of *la Nouvelle Vague* (the New
Wave) and all the way to the current French excellence in animation,
the French have frequently been at the forefront of the world of film.

France has more movie theater screens than any other European
country,[1] as well as a sizable movie production scene.

However, while in the U.S. the movie industry is a thriving business,
in France it's a vastly rigged game, played with copious amounts of
taxpayers' money. The money is distributed (either directly or indirectly)
by *l'État français* through the Centre National du Cinéma, different
regions, tax credits, tax loopholes, industry trade groups, and so forth
in amounts well into the nine digits per year. In France, approximately
€400 million of taxpayers' money are generously given away each year,
officially to support *le septième art* (the seventh art).[2]

In reality, however, as in most systems where massive amounts of

---

1 *"Les Français, plus gros consommateurs de cinéma en Europe,"* *AltusMedia Publicité*, www.express
roulartaservices.fr/les-francais-plus-gros-consommateurs-de-cinema-en-europe/.
2 *"Cinéma: les acteurs les plus arrosés par les subventions,"* *Capital*, May 12, 2015, www.capital.fr/en
quetes/revelations/cinema-les-acteurs-les-plus-arroses-par-les-subventions-1038205.

public money are injected, the reality is slightly less poetic: lack of financial accountability, a sense of self-importance, and systemic *copinage* (cronyism) abound. The result: films that are—surprise, surprise—expensive to make! Your average French movie costs €5.4 million (about $6.1 million) to make, as compared with an average €3 million (about $3.4 million) for an independent American movie. One of the most striking examples of this system is the silly amount of money paid to leading French actors: a well-known French producer recently broke the omertà and revealed how a French actor can be paid five times more in France than in the U.S. for a production that generates ten times less revenue.[3] Same goes for leading directors: a French B-lister like Philippe Lioret can be paid far more for a movie than American A-listers like Steven Soderbergh or Darren Aronofsky. It does seem fair indeed that an Alsatian plumber or a Normand baker's tax money would be used to cut huge checks to people making unsuccessful movies.

Understanding where the money comes from and how it's distributed helps understand all the clichés associated with French films. The buffer of public money renders making successful movies less of a gamble—and less of an objective: if millions consider your typical French movie to be boring and pretentious, it is because there's a good chance it is. Why care so much about the audience when the financial ecosystem is one based vastly on obtaining public funds in order to reach a very cushy break-even point? Add to this the fact that public subsidies put a certain editorial spin on the choice of the movies being produced, and you'll find that more and more French movies come into existence because they are ultimately in line with the new official ideological bias of our times.

This fact explains the decline of French cinema, which now is primarily made not by striking talents or uncompromised artists, but instead primarily by conformists, neck benders, and schmoozers. Con-

---

3 Vincent Maraval, *"Les acteurs français sont trop payés!," Le Monde,* December 28, 2012, www.le monde.fr/a-la-une/article/2012/12/28/les-acteurs-francais-sont-trop-payes_1811151_3208.html.

sequently, while until the seventies French actors, directors, and movies were revered by most movie buffs in the world, it is no longer the case. A vast majority of recent French movies no longer impress (*Le Mépris*, 1963), they no longer provoke intelligently (*La Grande Bouffe*, 1973) or criticize profoundly (*Playtime*, 1967), they have ceased to launch gorgeous French actors (where are the Brigitte Bardots and the Alain Delons of the 2000s?) or offer inspiring dialogues (*Les Tontons Flingueurs*, 1963).

As is frequently the case in France, the domestic movie industry is a good example of how public money, while typically used for goals presented as noble, is captured by a small group that profits from it while conveying—often obviously so—the narrative that the people cutting the checks wish to push onto the general public.

Ideas for a few relatively recent French movies worth watching, followed by their English-language titles where available:

COMEDIES
Intouchables (*The Untouchables*)
Le dîner de cons (*The Dinner Game*)
Le Père Noël est une ordure (*Santa Claus Is a Stinker*)
Les Bronzés (*French-Fried Vacation*)

DRAMAS
La maladie de Sachs (*Sachs' Disease*)
Les choristes (*The Chorus*)
De battre mon coeur s'est arrêté (*The Beat That My Heart Skipped*)

DOCUMENTARIES
Être et avoir (*To Be and to Have*)
Tabarly
Solutions locales pour un désordre global (*Think Global, Act Rural*)
Microcosmos (*Microcosmos*)

THRILLERS

Ne le dis à personne (*Tell No One*)

Mesrine: L'ennemi public #1 (*Mesrine: Public Enemy #1*)

OTHER

Le fabuleux destin d'Amélie Poulain (*Amélie*)

Bernie (*Bernie*)

Useful tip: French movies that make it overseas are usually worth it.

Sound like a French person: *"Je préfère les films américains. Les films français, c'est bon quoi . . . ultra chiants!"* (I prefer American movies. French movies are such a drag . . . so boring!)

THE ENGLISH 180

A few years ago, the French did not care much to speak English. They valued their language and culture and viewed it as strong enough that there was no point going through the hassle of having to speak (or learn) the language of their British archnemeses.

This very French mix of ignorance, attachment to the past, and misplaced arrogance bewildered many foreigners and gave the French a well-deserved reputation.

However, those days are long gone. When it comes to the English language, France has done a complete 180 as of late. Speaking English is no longer suspicious or traitorous—to millions it has become edgy and cool.

When interacting with foreigners, most French people will now be very eager to switch to English right away. Younger French people are particularly keen to display their English skills. The fact that most speak, understand, or write it rather terribly is irrelevant. Who cares about grammar when you can be cool?

The world of French media adopted words like *news, fashion, people,* and *stars* while the French corporate world has adopted *feedback, slides, boss,* and *meeting*—among many, many more such examples.

One of the most amusing consequences of this phenomenon is titles of American movies. While a few years back the majority of these titles were translated, and occasionally poorly so, it is now less and less frequently the case. For example, *Star Wars* came out in France under the title *La guerre des étoiles* (one star and several wars in English; several stars and one war in French). Even better: a recent French phenomenon is that more and more American (or British) movies in France are given a different, more simplistic English title.

Original Title	Title in France
The Hangover	*Very Bad Trip*
Silver Linings Playbook	*Happiness Therapy*
Knight and Day	*Night and Day*
Runaway Bride	*Just Married*
Date Night	*Crazy Night*
Killers	*Kiss & Kill*
Get Him to the Greek	*American Trip*
Youth in Revolt	*Be Bad*
Anger Management	*Self-Control*
The Best Exotic Marigold Hotel	*Indian Palace*
School of Rock	*Rock Academy*
Phone Booth	*Phone Game*
Into the Storm	*Black Storm*

Dumbed-down and simplified English, pronounced with a fabulously French accent, is growing to be the new official language at French movie theaters. Now English surely lures a number of French people. But add the word *sex* to the equation and you have yourself a real attention catcher.

Original Title	Title in France
No Strings Attached	Sex Friends
Not Another Teen Movie	Sex Academy
EuroTrip	Sex Trip
Wild Things	Sex Crimes
What's Your Number?	(S)ex List
Step Up	Sexy Dance

Ultimately, English in France is cool. Therefore, it sells.

Advertising in France has caught on to this phenomenon and has been introducing more and more campaigns with English terms. The epitome of this phenomenon and its efficiency can be seen in one of the strongest advertising campaigns of the past decade in France: George Clooney sipping on a cup of Nespresso, looking deep into the eye of the camera, and with his deepest, sexiest voice, saying, "What else?" The result: one billion cups of Nespresso are now drunk in France each year. France accounts for 25 percent of Nespresso's business worldwide.

A *star hollywoodienne* speaking to them in English is not something most French people are physically or mentally equipped to resist.

One might think that the result of this new French obsession with English would be a vastly improved command of the English language in France. Not quite: in Europe these days, it turns out, no other country speaks English as poorly as the French![1]

Many foreigners feel upset or disappointed when their attempts at speaking French in France are met with responses in English. They assume the French lack patience or appreciation, but in reality, they simply underestimate how cool English has become on Gallic soil!

---

1 Marion Senant, *"Niveau d'anglais: les Français derniers du classement européen,"* Cadremploi, November 17, 2014, www.cadremploi.fr/editorial/formation/langues/detail/article/niveau-danglais-les-francais-derniers-du-classement-europeen.html.

Useful tip: When speaking English with a French person, it's always best to use "international English" (slower enunciation, more simple vocabulary).

Sound like a French person: *"Lui, il parle américain, non?"* (He speaks American, right?)

AFRICANIZATION

𝒜 vast majority of the immigrants who have established themselves in France since the 1970s originate from Africa. Among immigrants of African descent living in France, there are two main categories of origins:

- Arabs from North Africa (Algeria, Morocco, Tunisia)
- Blacks from sub-Saharan Africa (Senegal, Ivory Coast, Mali, Gabon, Benin, etc.)

There exists a counterintuitive assumption in France that comfortably concludes that an African family moving to France will soon enough—through the almost magical merits of *l'universalisme républicain*—be essentially as French as a family who's been in France for centuries. As if moving somewhere made you forget your language, your roots, your favorite food, your religion, and your values. As if French society were so incredibly effective at integrating newcomers and introducing them to traditional French values and customs that all the traits of these immigrants' cultures of origin would not be passed on to the next generation.

The reality is, of course, extremely different. Firstly, over the past few decades, immigration to France has been a mass phenomenon. Both the volume of people and the speed with which they arrive have been staggering. Secondly, there is a huge diversity of origins. Tunisians are not Algerians, Senegalese are not Malians, and Algerians are certainly not Senegalese. Not to mention, of course, that Chinese are not Moroccans either. Importing populations also means importing preexisting racial, cultural, and religious practices as well as prejudices, biases, and conflicts.

Thirdly, there is an intrinsic malfunction of the French integration machine. With large numbers of immigrants flocking to affordable, immigrant-heavy neighborhoods, de facto ghettos came into existence. In France, many people of African descent live in neighborhoods and send their children to schools that most French people of French descent have deserted. So it is almost impossible for those children of immigrants to learn more about traditional French culture, values, and principles.

Consequently, the face of many parts of France has changed tremendously over the past few years. In short, many parts of France are home to entire neighborhoods mostly populated by blacks and Arabs.

In those neighborhoods, first-generation immigrants still wear traditional African clothing, salons naturally specialize in black beauty and hair, cafés are patronized by men only, veiled women are seen on every street, butcher shops sell halal meat, kebab shops flourish, mosques are built to accommodate the Muslim population, and so on. In France, the subject of Islam is often a topic of discussion, but the changing and increasingly African characteristics of the territory never are. Focusing on the consequence has become mainstream; acknowledging the principal cause, not quite.

Just as it is illusory to claim that moving to France makes you French, it would be incorrect to say that people of African descent born or raised in France remain completely Algerian or Senegalese, etc. To the extent that a great number of these disparate cultures share similar concerns, frustrations, aspirations, and, more important, references in the form of rap music with low-income populations in the United States, it is fair to assess that these areas are Africanized just as much as they are Americanized. When the fast-food chain Quick announced recently that it would switch to halal meat, many expressed concern over this step toward *l'islamisation*. What very few realized was the irony that consisted of the Islamization of France's Americanization.

The face of the French territory slowly but surely changes. While most cities, towns, and neighborhoods have grown to be multiethnic (to different degrees), some are not: some are more or less devoid of white French people. Glimpses of this can be seen, for instance, when taking the RER commuter train, which connects Paris to its surrounding *banlieues*, to reach an airport or convention center. People coming from the countryside tend to feel a deep shock—"*C'est fou, on est les seuls blancs dans tout le wagon*" (It's crazy. We're the only whites in this train car). The main question that typically comes to mind of the white person at that stage is: "Gosh, am I racist for thinking this?" Questions like "How did this happen?" don't seem to form often.

Ultimately, what the visible ethnic transformation of France reveals is the extent of the dispossession at hand and the impressive dilution of the French culture. It goes to show how profoundly the *"de souche"* ("native") French population has lost most of its mental antibodies: patriotism, sense of cultural identity, and willingness to address real issues have become extremely rare traits in France.

It's interesting to take a step back and look at the general context and the bigger picture: the population of Africa is booming (there were 100 million Africans in 1900, there are 1 billion today, and projections announce 2.5 billion Africans by 2050), while that of Europe is aging and not renewing itself. Considering that most mainstream political parties in Europe (left or right) are in favor of mass immigration and that the European Union has deprived member states of both borders and their right to control their immigration, there is no doubt that the ethnic and cultural compound of Europe in the coming years is bound to change even more radically.

Useful tip: Touchy subject!

Sound like a (young) French person: *"Wallah, téma les babtous!"* (Wallah, look at the whiteys!) *Babtou* is *verlan* for *toubab,* which in several parts of Africa refers to a person of European descent.

THE CONCEPT OF
MINISTRE

$\mathscr{P}$resident, vice president, secretary of state.

Key personnel in a U.S. administration is rather straightforward. The French, it is understood, do not specialize in straightforward.
That is even more true of French politicians.

Upon nominating his prime minister, the elected French president
asks him to form *un gouvernement*, generally referred to as "his government." In France, a *gouvernement* is comparable to what Americans
would refer to as "an administration" (as opposed to "the government"):
it is fully partisan and changes every few months or years, based on
the latest political escapades. Each government is made up of a prime
minister and the *ministres* he appoints.

So what is a *ministre*? On paper, a minister (the word has no religious
connotation in French) is the person in charge of a *ministère*, or
ministry—that is, a branch of the French government. Some major
ministries include the Ministry of the Economy, the Ministry of Education, the Foreign Ministry, and so on. Each ministry is a bureaucracy
in its own right, with its own responsibilities, employees (some of them
in the six- to seven-digit salary bracket), revenues, and budget. The
minister is in charge of implementing the respective aspects of the
executive's plan.

One may think *ministres* are picked based on their skills and experience—that a career diplomat typically gets appointed as foreign minister, or that a successful businessperson traditionally heads the Ministry of the Economy. Oh . . . you dreamer you, you silly idealist!

If the function of *ministre* has lost most of its glow over the past few decades, it is primarily because competence and legitimacy have become far less crucial in nominating *ministres* than the most blatant of buddy systems. Evidently, making it to the top means you (or your party) owe a lot of people a lot of favors. The easiest way to scratch the backs of the people who've scratched yours on your way up—or of those who might have dirt on you—is to nominate them as *ministres.* Easy and free . . . what's not to like? This incestuous system that consistently brings the worst apparatchiks to the top of the French executive makes your weekly Conseil des Ministres look like a rather interesting bunch of political friends, ex-lovers, and actual foes, all talking pompously about subjects they know close to nothing about.

Ministers typically operate out of stunning historical buildings, where they are treated like semiroyalty by their self-appointed court cabinet. *Monsieur le Ministre* this, *Madame la Ministre* that. The minister and his cabinet preside over the destiny of their ministry and its many employees. Perks typically include twenty-four/seven chauffeur service, full-time security (up to twenty guards at once), cushy salaries, free first-class travel, free lavish housing . . . It is time to finally cash in all these years of depressing political meetings and obscure rallies.

While certain *ministères* are the immutable pillars of any French government, others seem to come and go, making one wonder about their very relevance. One government has a health ministry; the next one doesn't. Does the health of French people get better or worst? You be the judge!

Some Americans worried about their political system rightly criticize the rampant system of revolving doors whereby Americans politicians in charge of a given regulatory agency become company execs in that very industry, and vice versa. Child's play. Revolving doors in France don't even bother with the private sector. Who needs shareholders, accountability, and clients anyway? French politicians have long understood that real luxury lies in otherwise extinct privileges and in the downright absence of true constraints: one day education minister, the next defense minister.

Any experience in education? Or the military?

Certainly not. But I did go to school with the prime minister!

Most politicians in France are career politicians. A good number of the most prominent ones have never held a real job. Every time their party gains control of the parliament, they're back for a new round, running a new Ministry of Whatever. What happens in between? The French system makes it possible to earn a comfortable living being paid as a vaguely elected official at one of the multiple local (municipal, departmental, regional), national (Assemblée Nationale, Sénat), or supranational (Strasbourg, Brussels) levels. Add the bogus commissions and the money the party pays its key people, and you've got yourself a whole career pretending to serve the people while taking advantage of them.

The more obvious the contempt for taxpayers and electors becomes, the greater the frustration and the anger against the political class grow among the French. When thinking of the structure of government in their country, a majority of French people these days now struggle to see beyond the striking incompetence and the obscene mismanagement. If you look at the results of the past few decades, it is hard to blame them.

There is very little doubt that new *ministères* will soon be created to pretend to address this burning issue. Prompt resolution surely is around the corner.

Useful tip: Serious fighting has been going on these past few years over whether a female minister was to be referred to as *Madame le Ministre* (masculine, referring to the function of *ministre*, which is a masculine noun) or the newer *Madame la Ministre* (technically mistaken in proper French but more satisfying to many).

Sound like a French person: "*Lui, il est passé de la santé à la défense. C'est vraiment du grand n'importe quoi!*" (So let me get this straight. He was in charge of public health, and now he's in charge of the military. This truly is grandiosely preposterous!)

PESSIMISM AND
NEGATIVITY

When it comes to pessimism, France can take any other country on earth.

In 2010, the French consumed more than 130 million sleeping pills and antidepressants.[1] They are the most morose people on earth—more pessimistic than even the people of Afghanistan and Iraq.[2] Only 5 percent of French youngsters consider the future to be promising.[3]

Pessimism in France ought to be viewed as a form of asceticism. The French have grown to expect nothing. While this belief could unveil to them the path to wisdom, it typically unveils instead the path to mild pessimism, because when the French expect nothing, what they truly expect is nothing good. Nothing bad is no longer a common horizon in the French psyche. The positive, joyful outlook once shared by older generations—the famous *joie de vivre*—is disappearing at a fast pace. While some elderly French ladies will still

---

1 *"État des lieux de la consommation de psychotropes en France,"* AFSSAPS Report, 2012.

2 Gallup International survey of expectations for 2012, cited in Simon Kuper, "A Nation of Pessimists," *Financial Times*, May 5, 2012, www.ft.com/cms/s/2/040e00aa-94b7-11e1-bb0d -00144feab49a.html#axzz489edbCET.

3 *"Les jeunesses face à l'avenir: une enquête internationale,"* Fondation pour l'Innovation Politique, www .fondapol.org/etude/221/.

smile at you on the street with kindness and benevolence, chances are their granddaughters are offering to the passerby nothing but a frown. France went from being a glass-half-full to a glass-half-empty society.

After World War II, the future was looking bright, heralding more peace and prosperity for all. But now the paradigm has shifted. Most people over the past few decades have witnessed a turn for the worst in their country. And if many French people can't resolve themselves to acknowledging it, there is no doubt that the grimness of collective perspectives contributes to their low morale.

Most French people more or less consciously view France as a sinking ship. And while the upkeep of a certain quality of life typically exists at a personal level, the French have grown rather hopeless when it comes to their collective destiny. In short, French people see their country slipping away, and most don't see an out.

The French grumble, rant, and complain unendingly. But they rarely do anything decisive about their problems. Complaining but not doing anything to make things better is a formidably French specialty. France is home to millions of negative crybabies who somehow believe that feeling sorry for themselves is a small yet meaningful step toward the resolution of their issues.

Voltaire once wrote, *"Il est poli d'être gai"*—It is polite to be joyful. However, most French people seem to have lost track of that basic form of courtesy. Countless French interactions are articulated around a succession of facts twisted negatively.

The weather's terrible?
Il pleut, il fait froid: c'est horrible! (It's cold, it's raining—it's horrible!)

The weather's beautiful?
Qu'est-ce qu'il fait chaud, c'est insupportable. (It's so hot, it's unbearable.)

It is helpful to understand that small talk in France is based on negative platitudes. That is how French people socialize and engage: by talking about how bad things, people, or places are. Do not approach a French person telling them you're in a great mood. They will look at you with suspicion. Instead, tell them how exhausted you are and you will have them engaged right away.

Moi aussi, j'suis épuisé! (Me too—I'm spent!)

It is an understatement to stress that, unlike in many other countries, a positive attitude is rarely the default attitude in France. This negative outlook on most things corresponds to a form of mental laziness, which is all the more toxic as it makes people feel smarter and more in the know than optimists and positive people.

It is a well-known fact that breakthroughs, discoveries, and tremendous success are indeed the exclusive domain of pessimists and negative people.

Useful tip: Don't let them get to you!

Sound like a French person: *"Mouais, ça m'étonnerait quand même. Si c'était une bonne idée, quelqu'un l'aurait déjà fait!"* (Nah . . . I doubt it. If it were a good idea, someone would have done it by now.)

EATING RULES

One of the most disturbing aspects of French culture for foreigners visiting France is the many rules that preside over the delicate art of meal eating in France.

First off, compared with many other nations, France has rather strict eating times. Trying to grab an early lunch or a late dinner is virtually impossible in most of the country. Throughout France, most restaurants will typically be closed outside the twelve p.m.–to–two thirty p.m. and seven p.m.–to–nine p.m. windows. Foreign patrons struggle to understand this phenomenon. Americans in particular, who are used to being served all day, generally see no good reason for restaurants to be shuttered. Frequently, when told, *"Désolé, la cuisine est fermée"*— Sorry, the kitchen is closed—they feel like French restaurateurs are conspiring against them or deliberately refusing to serve *les Américains*.

The reality is quite different: French people very rarely eat outside their traditional eating times, so there is no real point in keeping kitchen and service staff on deck. All the more so as French fiscal and labor laws make it such that operating a restaurant is very expensive and it is in the interest of the business to operate only one shift (eight hours, including prepping), covering both lunch and dinner, thus drastically limiting opening hours. French restaurateurs are not inhospitable, lazy, or obtuse. They are just operating on very tight budgets, no thanks to the French government.

Another French specialty that bewilders most foreigners is the amount of time French people spend at the dinner table. Eating quickly on the go has surely gained tremendous traction lately in France, particularly for weekday lunches, and yet any occasion the French have to indulge in a three- or four-hour meal they are known to seize enthusiastically.

Your typical French meal is a beautiful cultural construction. It is centered on three critical phases: *l'entrée, le plat principal, et le dessert*—appetizer, main course, dessert. French people will view a meal as incomplete if one of the three is missing. Most people sitting down at a French restaurant will therefore opt for *le menu,* a three-course affair that will typically have you in there for well above an hour. If the occasion is festive or the company agreeable, things commonly drag on for much longer: things start with an *apéritif* and occasionally finish with a *digestif.* All of a sudden, your ninety-minute, three-course operation turns into a four-hour, five-stage ordeal. In the company of a group of French people, most foreigners struggle with the three-course-menu culture. Foreigners are typically used to ordering one item based on their mood, desire, or availability. Ordering one steak or one salad when the rest of the diners go for *le menu* surely leads to a certain amount of discomfort.

That cultural difference culminates when foreigners decide to enter a French restaurant "just to get dessert." This triggers a mental malfunction in most French restaurant people—the idea is so preposterous that servers typically have to go ask both the manager and the chef. Everyone in the restaurant is as disoriented as if they had been asked to perform a dance atop the tables. "Just dess—? What? But? It's not poss—? Who? Hold on?"

Mental exhaustion quickly culminates. The awkwardness of the request introduces a major bug in their French meal matrix. The incident will be recounted for many months to friends and family.

L'autre jour, des Américains sont venus au restaurant et ont demandé juste un dessert! (The other day some Americans came to the restaurant and they only ordered a dessert!)

Major French hilarity typically ensues.
Take that, weirdo foreigners.

Useful tip: Elbows on the table in France are a no-no!

Sound like a French person: *"Tu vas prendre un poisson après une terrine quand même?"* (You can't have a fish as a main if you're having pâté as an appetizer.)

LES INTELLECTUELS

The French—there is no doubt about it—have a particular liking for ideas, words, and concepts. Conceptualizing and debating resonate to the very core of what it means to be French. Unlike facts, ideas are malleable: they can be crafted, twisted, romanticized . . . and they can make life more interesting.

From Voltaire to Sartre or Foucault, France has a tradition of high-flying thinkers whose intellectual contributions have, over the past centuries, become deeply embedded in not just French culture, but also philosophical, historical, and literary discourse throughout the entire world. The French have a special place in their hearts—and in their dinner parties—for never-ending discussions, often name-dropping those previously mentioned French intellectual luminaries. Every French town or village celebrates the most obscure of writers who happened to have spent time—be it only a few weeks—in their munic-ipality. The French take great pride in this. Plaques galore.

However, these days it has become obvious that the mold is bro-ken when it comes to intellectuals in France. Surely, the world we live in has become less interested in ideologies; experts and technicians seem to hold more relevant insights than those who dwell in abstraction. The glow surrounding intellectuals in France has swiftly diminished recently, with no one to take up the mantles of the great thinkers.

Who are today's intellectuals in France? It is hard to say. Surely books are being written, newspaper articles are being published, televised debates are being had. But who shines a true light? Who rises higher than all the rest? Who proposes a coherent comprehensive vision? The relevance of the work of an intellectual also lies in whether his thoughts alter the course of existence or of the world. To that extent, looking into "intellectuals" these days implies looking into airtime and publicity.

To the general public, French intellectuals could be divided into conservative and liberal, into left wing and right wing. Partaking, however, in manufactured, frequently dated, and generally inoffensive debates is not the domain of brilliant intellectuals but that of *intellectuels officiels*. Those are given airtime. Militants with a cause posing as intellectuals may fool the masses—they surely have and will. Boring debates occur before the general public—surely not enlightening, but indeed reassuring.

Of course, questions are rarely posed about which debaters are getting paychecks from whom. Nevertheless, this is essential to understanding the apparent decline in France's ability to produce and nurture a new generation of intellectuals. When the main official debaters won't touch certain subjects, when researchers with dissenting views are never invited to the table, the quality of the subsequent exchange of ideas will simply plateau. With nothing of substance to discuss, these spectacles are meaningless.

Having entered a new era in which some thinkers are blacklisted from public discussions for having views considered by the shot-callers as too radical, France is now home to a cast of *intellectuels dissidents*. These are the unofficial intellectuals—people given no airtime, people whose understanding, analyses, criticisms, or ideas are not acceptable ones to spread according to the people controlling the media. To that extent, France is starting to resemble the USSR. In France, historians may be thrown in jail for what they write.[1] Certain French intellectuals do offer compelling analyses and consequently develop significant online followings, but if they are not politically correct, they will likely be treated with disdain by most people in the media, in the corporate world, or in academia.

The passion of French people in the realm of ideas still shows online. A quick visit to YouTube reveals that a self-proclaimed *intellectuel dissident* like Alain Soral has a strong following; his videos, in which he pontificates for hours about politics, geostrategy, and literature, reach hundreds of thousands of views. Being vocally anti-Zionist and generally too much of a provocateur for what the French press has become, he's persona non grata in all French media. Étienne Chouard, who advocates banning parties and substituting elections by drawing is in a similar situation. With such ideas, he's not invited on TV often! Incidentally, the one time he made it to a mainstream TV show, his four-minute tirade went viral online, breaking the taboo and telling the general public that politicians were not—as many believe—incompetent fools, but smart puppets doing a terrific job of serving the interests of the ones paying for their campaigns.

Given the general inadequacy and one-sidedness of the official intellectual debates in France, a growing number of French are hungry for more. They seek online what they can't find in traditional mainstream media.

Thankfully, the romantic figure of the French intellectual is therefore not dead; he is just smothered.

---

1 http://www.lemonde.fr/societe/article/2015/02/11/le-negationniste-vincent-reynouard-de-nouveau-condamne-a-la-prison-ferme_4574671_3224.html.

Useful tip: *Intello* is how an intellectual person is often referred to by all family members: *l'intello de la famille.*

Sound like a French person: *"Oh moi, ces intellectuels qui nous font la leçon, je peux pas les supporter. C'est simple, je coupe, maintenant."* (I just can't stand these "intellectuals" anymore—always acting superior. I just tune it out now.)

THE YOUNG-BOY HAIRCUT

Very few social norms in France are embraced as widely as the young-boy haircut rule. While it has to do with a deeply ingrained, uniquely French sense of social decency, this standard behavior generally goes entirely unnoticed and is rarely spoken about. Even in France.

What is it about? Very simply: past a certain age, all Frenchwomen adopt the same haircut—which, incidentally, they share with young boys age five to nine years old.

There is rarely an exception to this rule. However, the ubiquitous style is still customizable in three specific ways:

- **Coloring:** As in most countries, two schools of thought exist among Frenchwomen: dyed vs. natural hair color. It should be noted that a surprisingly large number of elderly French ladies—no doubt among the pro-coloring set—walk the streets sporting, through some cosmetic miracle, inexplicably purple hair.

- **Length:** Nature's gifts and a woman's monthly salon budget are the key defining elements of hair length. While "short" is a given and not left to discussion, just how short and how stylish are still the woman's choice.

- **Age:** There is a point in a Frenchwoman's life at which she will deem that she is too old to have long hair. There are very few exceptions to this rule. The tipping point is often related to both the lady's self-confidence and her level of self-consciousness.

The young-boy haircut is the corollary to one unpublicized, yet undeniable, general truth about women's hairstyling in France: less is . . . enough. When it comes to haircuts, Frenchwomen do specialize in "good enough."

The general philosophy of not overdoing it transforms into not doing much in day-to-day life. While hairstyles that reflect the wearers' personality and unique style sensibilities are not uncommon in the United States, the French generally opt for a style that simply works. The ratio of efforts to total cost to visual effect usually leans more toward minimization than maximization. This will ironically have Francophile Americans raving about the raging elegance of Frenchwomen.

It comes, therefore, as no surprise that when witnessing the loss of their hair's youthful qualities, most Frenchwoman adopt an undeclared "screw it" approach, thus taking their minimalist coiffure philosophy to a whole new level.

As with any widely spread social norm, no explanation is really needed. If challenged, two main reasons are held up in defense:

- *C'est plus pratique* (It's more practical) is the usual explanation. The convenience card—who can argue with that?

- *J'ai passé l'âge* (I'm beyond the age . . .) is the line used by women who are no longer playing games. Translation: I'm old and through with the fuss—beat it.

While American Francophiles will compliment Frenchwomen who "age gracefully," Frenchmen don't always have the distance to see it that way. Their life partner's young-boy haircut is not something up for discussion. At some point in life, it just is. Like a seed gently planted in their subconscious: *Honey,* it says, *you're not getting younger either!*

Useful tip: The word *brushing* is used in French with a different meaning: *J'ai fait un brushing* means "I got a blow-dry."

Sound like a French person: *"Y a un âge pour tout!"* (At a certain age, there are some things you just no longer do!)

THE RISE OF THE
FRONT NATIONAL

Over the past two decades, in France as in other Western countries, it has become apparent to more and more people that there are very few differences remaining between so-called right-wing and left-wing political movements.

The alternating of leaders, administrations, and governments has made it increasingly obvious that Western politicians are but mere actors enforcing the visions and wishes of the powers that be. No matter which "side" is in office, some constants remain: more debt (hence more control), more immigration (hence more tensions), more supranational government (hence less genuine democracy), less quality education (hence a less enlightened populace), etc.

Politicians, of course, work hard at making it look as if their views and policies are deeply distinct from those of the other camps and rival parties. They turn petty subjects into wedge issues constantly. The French media—just like other mainstream media abroad—relentlessly reinforce the impression of veracity regarding the puppet show.

Just as much as its tragic and ominous consequences, the obscene farce has led to the rise of a third major party: the Front National, currently headed by Marine Le Pen. While *le FN* was established in 1972, it has only gained ground to become a key political force over the past decade. For most of its voters, it is perceived as the only real alternative to the perceived threat of imminent collapse.

While the French media did a tremendous job of associating the party with neutral-sounding keywords like *extrême droite*, *racisme*, and *fascisme*, in most countries of the globe the Front National's platform would correspond to that of a moderate left-wing party: reasoned protectionism, pro-sovereignty, anti–mass immigration, and in favor of the government controlling health care, education, banking, and energy.

Since the so-called left has fully abandoned the French working class, it only makes sense for a significant proportion of the French working class to entrust the Front National with their ballot. For Front National voters, there is little doubt that the constant letdowns and incessant moralizing of the political and media classes have slowly but surely led them to, as the French media puts it, *basculer à l'extrême droite* (switch over to the extreme right). These working-class citizens are thinking, "I've had it. We need to get rid of these unbearable crooks who are ruining this country. Let's try something else—can't be worse than what we have."

Over the past few years, Marine Le Pen and her team worked on the *dédiabolisation* (the "undemonizing" or mainstreaming) of the party. The party has to gain respectability and stop coming across as racist, fascist, or dangerous to a majority of the population in order to gain a real foothold. Whether this objective is being reached or not is anybody's guess. In the meantime, the French media and political class present the Front National as the ultimate enemy to democracy with a level of intensity, relentlessness, and frequency that is almost laughable. The fact that the media and politicians that both fight to defend and fully embody that so-called democracy are the very incarnation of its non-existence is irrelevant. "Democracy is in danger" surely sounds more compelling than "Keep voting as we're telling you to."

Useful tip: If you understand French, the analyses of François Asselineau on the Front National are quite interesting.

Sound like a French person: *"Non, mais le FN, quand même c'est pas possible, y a des limites."* (The FN—no, really, that's impossible. I just won't go there. There are some lines I won't cross.)

COMMUNAL SONGS

*V*ery few things say "Europe" as much as a good old communal song. Whether regional classics, traditional chants, goofy songs, party essentials, or pop culture classics, there is no shortage of good old songs that call for communal singing.

Truth be told, blending into genuine French culture does not require the mastery of French culture, French language, or French traditions. All it takes is the ability to enunciate the following three syllables: *la-la-la.*

Once that feat is achieved, all you need is patience. Well, patience and booze. Give enough time to any drinking French group and enjoy the mild delight of witnessing the men break into some sort of singing ritual.

This phenomenon is undoubtedly exacerbated within certain chant-rich subcultures: sailors, rugby people, military personnel, *grandes écoles* students and alumni . . . all have their end-of-dinner songs and most people will know the lyrics to their particular tunes. Most of them even know the actual words!

The ratio of actual words to *la-la-la* diminishes when a regional chant breaks out. Most locals are usually familiar with the tune, but many will have only a vague command of the words (or the dialect).

Some regional chants have straight up given up on words and made *la-la-la* the official lyrics. Such as Burgundy's *"Ban bourguignon"*—on a visit to Burgundy, should you walk into a rousing chorus of the *"Ban bourguignon"* at the end of a dinner, don't show ignorance by assuming you walked into a drunken symposium of mentally retarded French people. What you're witnessing is not collective mental retardation—it's French culture!

Should a group dinner not give way to communal singing, again, patience should apply. The next stage of the evening invariably will. As French people hit the dance floor, one thing is bound to happen: the spontaneous formation of a communal singing circle. When a favorite song comes on, one person will wrap his arm around a friend's shoulder, that friend will do the same, and then, within seconds, in a move as swift as it is surreptitious, the dance floor becomes a ritualistic round characterized by the hypnotic repetition of the same mysterious sequence of sounds: *lalala*.

At this stage, the round might take several forms. The rotating-round is of course the ultimate classic, but other options do exist: the alternating-dancer-in-the-middle is another favorite, the each-side-moves-back-and-forth being the third main option. After each verse, for one to five sentences the *la-la-la*-ing is replaced by the chorus that everybody in the circle knows. Should the chorus be in English, it is fully acceptable, of course, given the time and the collective level of intoxication, to *faire du yaourt*—use a form of made-up English-sounding mumbo jumbo.

The culture of communal singing is so deeply ingrained that it morphed from village chants a few decades ago to pop culture hits nowadays. And while the same megahits are played in parties from San Francisco to Bangkok, only in that strange country called France will they turn more often than not into communal singing opportunities.

The greatest moment of collective joy of the past decades in France was undoubtedly the World Cup victory of the national soccer team in the summer of 1998. One song (a cover of Gloria Gaynor's "I Will

Survive") became the anthem of the team and soon enough that of a generation. It should come as no surprise that the main lyrics for that song were: *la / la-la / la-la / la-la-la-la-la-la / la-la-la-la / la-la-la-la-la-la / la-la-la-la-la-la-laaaa / ah / la / la-la* . . .

Who said learning French was difficult?

Useful tip: If you're intrigued by songs that might be considered "funny, medieval, and kinky," look into *chansons paillardes*.

Sound like a French person: *"La chenille, allez, c'est la chenille! Françoise, Thierry, Marco, ramenez-vous, on fait la chenille!"* (Let's do the caterpillar, guys! Françoise, Thierry, Marco, get over here. Let's do the caterpillar!) The "caterpillar" is basically a French conga line.

TAXES

❦

$\mathcal{J}$hink your country is good at taxing its people? Your country is but a child!

With more than two hundred different sorts of taxes, my country can take your country any day. Does your country tax cross-country skiing, dying, and things made out of terra-cotta?[1] I didn't think so. Does it tax mineral water, plane tickets, and pylons?[2] Probably not.

Taxation is France's great game of creativity. Between 2010 and 2014, France created no fewer than forty-four new taxes.[3] The challenge for politicians is: what can we tax that has not been taxed yet? When imagination runs short, the challenge becomes less about imagination, more about bravado. In college, you played drinking games? French politicians probably still do, over lunch:

---

1 French General Tax Code—Article L2333-81; French General Tax Code—Article L2223-22; Decree No. 2000–1278, December 26, 2000, establishing a parafiscal tax on products made of concrete and earthen terra-cotta.
2 French General Tax Code—Article 1582; Act No. 2005-1720, December 30, 2005, financial amendment for 2005; French General Tax Code—Article 1519 A.
3 Marie-Cécile Renault, *"La France, championne du monde de la créativité fiscale,"* Le Figaro, March 31, 2015, www.lefigaro.fr/impots/2015/03/31/05003-20150331ARTFIG00373-la-france-championne-du-monde-de-la-creativite-fiscale.php.

Guys, whoever downs this last has to raise the income tax to
75 percent!

> Haaaaa . . . you're such an idiot! Let's do it!

Okay, ready? Three, two, one . . .

And there you go: 75 percent became the official taxation rate for high-earning individuals in France.[4] Now, if you earn a lot, drink a lot of Evian, like cross-country skiing, and the occasional terra-cotta thingy . . . well, you've officially become a major sponsor of the next drinking game!

In 2013, more than eight thousand French households paid over 100 percent of their taxable income in taxes.[5] Translation: all of what these people earned that year went to the tax man. And then some!

To understand the predicament of your typical French taxpayer, let's step in his shoes for a second. Imagine you're in France, living a normal life, working a normal job. Let's follow the money trail:

- At the end of the month, you get your paycheck. A significant fraction gets taken out immediately to pay for several social charges (on which more below). So only part of your paycheck actually makes it to your bank account. Fair enough.

- Now, every morning, you have to drive to work. Every time you fill up your tank, 56 percent of that goes to the tax man.[6] Did I mention the taxes you've already paid on your license plate and your driver's license?

---

4 *"Le Conseil constitutionnel valide la taxe à 75 percent," Libération,* December 29, 2013, www.libera tion.fr/economie/2013/12/29/le-conseil-constitutionnel-valide-la-taxe-a-75-sur-les-hauts-revenus _969484.

5 Emilie Lévêque, *"Comment peut-on payer plus de 100 percent d'impôts?," L'Express/L'Expansion,* May 21, 2013, http://lexpansion.lexpress.fr/actualite-economique/comment-peut-on-payer-plus-de -100-d-impots_1450870.html.

6 *"Structuration des prix de l'essence et du gazole (France)," Connaissance des Énergies,* www.connais sancedesenergies.org/fiche-pedagogique/structuration-des-prix-de-l-essence-et-du-gazole-france.

- After a long workday, you get home. After all, you do pay a tax on having a home—you demanding little thing.

- Now you're hungry, so you go to the store to buy food: 20 percent sales tax on that.

- You're exhausted. You turn on the TV. And why shouldn't you? It's your right: you do pay a tax every year for owning a TV.

- In the morning, you wake up. Bad luck—you overslept. When you get to your car, bummer—there's a parking ticket on the windshield. Attentive tax man, isn't he?

- Thankfully, next week you're on vacation. Detox: you'll be flying to the Alps to go cross-country skiing and drink lots of fresh mountain spring water: tax, tax, and retax!

Then, at the end of the year, you'll be required to kindly be a good citizen and contribute to public finances by, you guessed it: paying your taxes.

When it comes to comparing perks against taxes paid, a number of people like to argue, "Yes, but in France at least you get free health care." What these people usually don't know is that, in France, taxes do not go toward covering the cost of health care (known as *la sécurité sociale*, or *la sécu*). The cost of the universal health care system is covered by an additional system of taxation known as *les cotisations sociales* (also known as *les charges*, or social charges). More taxation! Heck, taxes cover only 60 percent of the monies collected by the French government. The rest—a staggering 40 percent—comes from these *cotisations sociales*. Adding taxes and social charges together reveals that the actual taxation rate on French companies is . . . wait for it . . . 64.7 percent.[7] While French companies are being taxed into oblivion, your *average—*

7 Isabelle de Foucaud, *"La France, championne d'Europe des charges sociales pesant sur les entreprises,"* Le Figaro, November 20, 2013, www.lefigaro.fr/impots/2013/11/20/05003-20131120ARTFIG00341-la-france -championne-d-europe-des-charges-sociales-pesant-sur-les-entreprises.php.

not rich—French employee typically pays over 55 percent of what he earns in taxes and charges of various forms.[8] Fifty-five percent! In short, when a company pays an employee €2,350 per month, once you deduct all taxes and charges paid by both parties, the employee is left with only €1,000.[9]

Depending on the exact rate, which varies from year to year and from person to person, 100 percent of what a French employee earns from January 1 to mid-July typically goes straight to the pockets of the ever-greedy French tax man.

Did somebody say "free" health care?

Useful tip: Don't start paying taxes in France.

Sound like a French person: *"Et les impôts locaux ont encore augmenté cette année. C'est quand même un truc de fou!"* (Local taxes have gone up again this year. It's truly mind-boggling.)

8 *"En France, plus de la moitié des revenus du travail partent en impôts, taxes et charges sociales,"* Capital, July 24, 2013, www.capital.fr/finances-perso/actualites/en-france-plus-de-la-moitie-des-revenus-du-travail-partent-en-impots-taxes-et-charges-sociales-860972.
9 Marine Rabreau, *"En France, pour 100 euros nets, il faut 235 euros de salaire 'super brut,'"* Le Figaro, July 29, 2015, www.lefigaro.fr/economie/le-scan-eco/dessous-chiffres/2015/07/29/29006-20150729ARTFIG00006-en-france-pour-100-euros-nets-il-faut-235-euros-de-salaire-super-brut.php.

LA CONVIVIALITÉ

$\mathcal{U}$nderstanding France requires having a good grasp of the concept of *convivialité*. *Con* "with"; *vivi* "life." *La convivialité* is what makes a person pleasant to be around. If we say, *"Jean-Claude, il est convivial,"* it means Jean-Claude is likable, approachable, warm, engaging, easy to be around. The French adjective *convivial* (pronounce it right now, will you?) is close to the English word "friendly" but also incorporates a degree of typical French *joie de vivre*. More specifically, this may entail a commitment to the so-called *plaisirs de la table*—having a good time while sharing a meal. Ask a French person to think of someone who is *convivial*, and chances are good that person will not be skinny! *La convivialité* has to do with an attitude as much as with an ever-present invitation to indulge in the small pleasures and the gentle excesses—liquid and solid—that make life more enjoyable.

Being *convivial* is understanding, accepting, and fully playing one's role as a *convive*—as a participant in what the Latin language referred to as a *convivium*, or shared meal. The English translation of *convive*—a diner—surely does not resonate with the same etymological and social charge. Conviviality has to do with the pleasure of being together, of making all the pieces of a great shared meal come together—from a love of good food to a taste for good wine to a particular knack for friendly and sincere conversations. *La convivialité* is a uniquely French notion, and the usage and meaning of the term have no direct equivalent in any other language, a testament to just how important eating and socializing are in France—how there can be no good conversation without food, and how good food without friends and dialogue is not worth much. Being *convivial* means having mastered this superior synthesis. The result: good times and good meals for those around.

Convivialité is so quintessential to French culture that the word can now refer to places in addition to people. It is therefore very common (and desirable) for a restaurant to be described as *convivial*. The atmosphere, the memories, the world of possibilities, the generosity, the choice of dishes—heck, maybe even the prices—all contribute to the beloved *atmosphère conviviale* the French adore.

Lately, in an interesting semiotic twist, the word has become a common translation in the IT world for what the English language refers to as "user-friendly." *Une plate-forme conviviale* is one that is easy to use. Oh, the friendliness of zeros and ones . . .

Useful tip: As the level of *convivialité* escalates (proportionally to the wine intake generally), it becomes completely okay to randomly tap people on the back or shoulder!

Sound like a French person: *"Un bon repas, c'est bien manger, bien boire, des amis et de la convivialité."* (A good meal means eating well, drinking well, some friends, and *convivialité*.)

LEAVING FRANCE

The number of French people living abroad has more than doubled over the past twenty years.[1] French people are leaving France at an unprecedented rate.

Oddly enough, the context of a country characterized by mass unemployment, striking negativity, a toxic ideology, mind-boggling over-regulation, rampant insecurity, and brutal taxation does not seem to appeal to some.

The French are strange like that.

Preferred destinations include London, Canada, Australia, the United States, Brazil, Asia, and also, more recently, certain Persian Gulf countries. Opportunities (real or perceived), language, proximity, and lifestyle are all key criteria for French folks choosing a new destination.

This phenomenon is startling among certain categories of the population, particularly the young and educated upper class, entrepreneurs, and general go-getters.

---

1 Benoît Floc'h, *"De plus en plus de jeunes quittent la France,"* Le Monde, March 10, 2014, www.lemonde .fr/economie/article/2014/03/10/de-plus-en-plus-de-jeunes-quittent-la- france_4380276_3234 .html.

In many French families, it has now become the new normal to have one or several children or grandchildren dispersed throughout the world.

Some young French people leave France with cotton-candy dreams, hoping to find a greener-grassed El Dorado, full of opportunities that will finally shine the light on the talent that their home country can't seem to honor. Those Kool-Aid drinkers tend to leave France with no hard skills or with degrees that don't translate overseas. They typically find themselves bewildered when other countries don't seem to have amazing high-paying and "interesting" jobs for them. These ones go back to France and tell their friends, *"C'est pas forcément mieux ailleurs"* (It's not necessarily better elsewhere). Their account of their experience usually ends stressing the all-important fact that France has "free health care." Traveling surely helps them gain a better understanding of how the world works.

For those, however, who have managed to build true competence and/or reach their new destination with the willingness to work hard and be humble, opportunities frequently tend to arise overseas. Among these French people who find satisfying jobs and/or living conditions, the number of those aspiring to return to France later in life is diminishing at a staggering pace. What is at stake here is not mere expatriation or experience seeking. What is at stake is called emigration.

Until very recently and for many decades, France had been a country of *im*migration—going *in*. People from other countries came to France seeking opportunities, safety, a good quality of life, and, of course, formidable lovers. While nearby Italy, Ireland, England, Poland, Spain, Portugal, and other European countries had known significant emigration of their peoples in the past decades and centuries, that hadn't been the case for France.

The country is currently undergoing its first emigration crisis since the (entrepreneurial) Protestant Huguenots left Louis XIV's Catholic France beginning in 1685. In hindsight, this turned out to be terrible news for France, but a great boon for England, South Africa, the United States, and Germany.

There is no doubt that, when it comes to regulation, fiscal matters, and opportunities, the grass is no doubt greener in many other countries on earth (and certainly worse in others). Still, it is essential to grasp, and address, the collective psychological context that leads hundreds of thousands of a country's most youthful, educated, and resourceful people to leave.

To many French people, France is lost. Its inability to reform itself (the job market), the constant worsening of key issues (fiscal, regulatory), and the degradation of the general quality of life (violence, impoverishment, unemployment) give some the sense that there is very little hope to be had for France. Most wouldn't even consider getting involved and trying to change society from the inside. After all, it does take having a job (for younger people) or enough free time and energy (for people who work). A majority of French politicians are *fonctionnaires* who have never worked in the private sector.

Ultimately, many French people feel that efforts in France are not rewarded and that society as a whole will generally crush, torment, ruin, criticize, and demoralize you if you're an honest, law-abiding, and hardworking citizen. If you happen to have or to make money, even worse. On the other hand, these same people notice the shocking difference in treatment and consideration, witnessing the free passes, free benefits, and undue advantages given to criminals and anyone (including many foreigners) who by choice or by circumstance do not participate in the collective effort to make a society work.

Consequently, France turns out to be perceived by an ever-growing number of French people as a sour, unfair, and ultimately insane place where hardworking French people get treated worse by their government than lawbreaking foreigners.

To the poorer individuals for whom leaving the country is not an option, hatred and resentment typically ensue—understandably. For those with enough cultural and financial resources to consider expatriation, a clean slate elsewhere usually sounds like a tempting option.

For millions of French people, the conclusion is that France is no longer a good or smart place to be. They will profusely—and rather Frenchly so—complain about it at every dinner party and every family reunion, encouraging anyone who can to leave *ce pays de cons* (this country of morons). The nephew who returns to France for the holidays will discreetly agree with his uncle's rant, and will be glad to leave France after a few days, for truly, as his uncle once again demonstrated over Christmas dinner: *"Les gens sont trop négatifs en France!"*—People are too negative in France!

It shall be noted that the phenomenon at hand does not touch all categories of French society: for instance, politicians—some may regret it—don't ever seem to leave.

Useful tip: More French restaurants, cafés, pastry shops, and bakeries opening near you soon!

Sound like a French person: *"Eh beh, son neveu, celui qui est parti vivre à Londres, figure-toi qu'il s'est marié avec une Allemande!"* (Well, her nephew, the one who moved to London, turns out he married a German girl!)

EFFEMINATE MEN

Saying that Frenchmen are effeminate is a trite platitude. However, like most clichés, it is grounded, at least somewhat, in reality.

There is no doubt that a foreigner walking the streets of Paris will be surprised at the puniness of the average Parisian male. Countless Parisians are shockingly deprived of basic muscle mass and apparently very uninterested in—or very unsuccessful at—developing any. Undoubtedly, architecture is not the only gift Paris has to offer: marveling at these skinny bodies no doubt adds a mysterious dimension to the memorable experience a proper exploration of Paris offers.

But what is true of Paris is not necessarily true outside Paris. While on average Frenchmen are not as meaty as American males, the degree of puniness typically drops outside Paris. Frenchmen come in all colors, shapes, and forms and, thankfully for Frenchwomen, not all of them look like your average Parisian. But on the whole, men's men are few and far between, since Frenchmen are seldom instructed to provide or to fight.

What is often overlooked in the cliché about effeminate Frenchmen is that it is not only a physical thing; today, it is primarily a psychological trait.

French society takes the recent Western trend toward women getting stronger and men getting weaker to another level entirely. In a society that keeps half its people living off government money and that fiscally incites the other half to build a life as an employee and not as an entrepreneur, an artist, or otherwise a truly self-reliant, independent being,[1] an immense majority of Frenchmen are wage earners. They live their lives in an emasculating system that has them working and waiting for a paycheck from somebody else while enduring their daily dose of small hypocrisies. The result of this sociological reality is that there are very few real men left in France. Most of the virility left on French territory is concentrated in the *banlieues,* where the feminization of men has not gained as much ground. Needless to say, this social and geographical polarization of testosterone distribution understandably preoccupies sagacious observers.

Useful tip: If you're interested in how French people "stay so skinny," don't forget to ask men too!

Sound like a French person: "Oh, t'as de gros muscles. T'es le plus fort! Ha ha!" (Oh, you've got big muscles. You're the strongest now, aren't you? Ha ha!)

---

1 http://www.eric-verhaeghe.fr/rsi-liberez-entrepreneurs/.

SMOKING

$\mathcal{F}$or years, I heard many Americans in Paris telling me with genuine incomprehension and real fear in their eyes: "It's crazy here. Everyone smokes."

My best answer was an uninspired smirk. As a young Frenchman, I didn't really think that "everyone" smoked. More like "some people" smoked, which seemed rather normal.

Last year, though, after having spent a few months in the United States, I returned to France and within days of being back couldn't help but think to myself . . . "It's crazy here. Everyone smokes!"

Merde!

Indeed, one is twice as likely to run into a smoker in France than in the United States (32 percent of adults smoke in France compared with 16 percent in the U.S.).[1] Among younger Frenchies (eighteen to thirty-four years old), the proportion of smokers escalates to 50 percent. A house party in France is basically another word for a smoke party: get that detergent ready, because those cool clothes you're wearing *will* smell rank in the morning.

---

1 *"Chiffres du Tabac," Tabac Info Service*, www.tabac-info-service.fr/Vos-questions-Nos-reponses /Chiffres-du-tabac.

In total, a typical French person spends months of his life suffering through conversations about smoking. It all starts in middle school, when conversations deal with the thrill: trying cigarettes (or not), hiding them from parents, buying them, finding a discreet place to smoke them after school. In high school, as smoking intensifies, discussions shift. It's called becoming more mature. The focus is now on the constant need for *une pause clope* (a cigarette break) and the best techniques to avoid your parents' suspicions about your newly developed habit. After high school, adult life in France is mostly a long succession of conversations about smokers' need to smoke and their need to stop smoking.

Life in France is fascinating like that.

The *pause clope* is a landmark moment of French culture. It all starts in high school, with quite the fascinating sight for the untrained eye: every two hours, outside every single French high school, hordes of kids suddenly flock to the sidewalk right in front of the school's entrance for five to ten minutes, just to smoke their cigarettes. When the bell rings again, they all scamper back inside.

Later in life, the cigarette break remains an institution. Just as in their earlier years, nonsmokers happily join smokers on their cigarette breaks. After all, why should they not get a break when their colleagues do? Good luck arguing with that one, boss man!

While since the 1960s the proportion of male smokers has dropped significantly in France, that of female smokers has surged. You go, girl—bridge that gender gap! Right after noticing, "It's crazy here. Everyone smokes," most American ladies usually add: "Even girls." Then they ask, "But why?," with fear in their eyes, suddenly turning to a mix of suspicion and jealousy, as they ask, "Is that how they stay thin?"

No matter how accustomed Frenchmen are to dissipating smoke screens, American women should realize that they know far more about a Frenchwoman than any Frenchman ever could.

Useful tip: Though illegal, weed consumption in France is massive.

Sound like a French person: *"Ouhh . . . ça sent la clope!"* (Ooh . . . smells like a cigarette!)

DIVORCE

Over the past few decades, all things related to family matters have evolved a great deal in France.

Starting with marriage. French people get married less or do so later in life: while in the 1960s the average age for marriage was twenty-four, it is now thirty-one (thirty-two for Frenchmen, thirty for French-women). These extra years to search for the right partner do not, however, seem to lead to a better success rate: the divorce rate is now over 52 percent, up from 10 percent in the early 1970s.

In short: France is now characterized by fewer marriages and more divorces.

In France, the odds of divorce peak after five years. If the divorcing couple has children, in 76 percent of cases full custody will be granted to the mother, while in only 15 percent will custody alternate between Mommy and Daddy.[1]

The notion of family structure has changed tremendously in France over the past decades: 10% of French children now live in a *famille re-*

---

1 Sources: INSEE and INED.

composée,[2] while more than 22% live in a *famille monoparentale*.[3] While it is losing its predominance, the *famille traditionnelle* model remains the main setup in which French people choose to raise their children.

Useful tip: If you're invited to a French wedding, be prepared for a (very) late night.

Sound like a French person: "Tu sais que Delphine a divorcé?" (Did you hear that Delphine got divorced?)

2 http://www.insee.fr/themes/document.asp?ref_id=ip1470.
3 http://www.terrafemina.com/societe/societe/articles/54676-familles-monoparentales-85-de-meres
-celibataires.html.

GRAY ZONES
IN THE LAW

$\mathcal{C}$ ulturally, in France, the law typically serves as more of a general guideline.

In most cases, complying is fine. However, sometimes the law is downright inconvenient. In these cases, most French people understand that it is okay to suspend their obedience to the law, just for a few seconds. The French do not consider suspending their adhesion to the rule of law an instance of actually breaking the law.

Both individually and collectively, they understand that, sometimes, breaking the law is just no big deal. The law in France is not viewed as a dividing line between black and white. Gray surely exists and that is where French people truly thrive.

One of the most peculiar things for a French person traveling to the United States is what is known as jaywalking. Jaywalking in France is called common sense. No cars? Go. French people jaywalk in front of police cars without thinking twice about it. French cops, being French, would have to be under some very strict orders to fine anyone for jaywalking right before their eyes.

The farther south one goes in France, the more creative the interpretation of the law becomes. For example, the farther south you go, the less reliable the credit card machines seem to be: *"Désolé, la machine est cassée"* (Sorry. The credit card machine's broken)—guess I'll have to pay in cash, then! In the South of France, charmingly inventive tricks are not rare: recently in Nice, for instance, a man put official-looking stickers on his minibus and started taking on passengers waiting for the bus and charging them for the ride![1] Why not?

The South of France is also home to the most well-known criminal organizations in the country. They are known as *Le Milieu* or *la pègre* and have historically been particularly active in Marseille, Nice, Corsica, and Toulon. This is old-school French criminality, depicted in the movie *The French Connection.* The new-school criminal organizations from France typically emanate from either the Gypsy community (for thefts) or from the *quartiers sensibles* (in the *banlieues*). Groups from the *banlieues* started in the very prosperous drug-trafficking business, focusing primarily on marijuana. Some graduated to extortion and killings. Foreign criminal groups also settled and started doing business in France—after all, globalization also works for gangsters. The level of activity has grown exponentially over the past decade: arms trafficking is controlled by groups from the Balkans, Albanians compete with Turks on the heroin market, Nigerians compete with people from the Balkans for the biggest share of the prostitution sector, Romanians specialize in metal theft, Georgians do well in robberies . . . Some organizations also use France to launder money. That is typically the case of Russian or Italian criminal groups that invest in high-end real estate in Paris, on the French Riviera, and in the French Alps.[2]

No criminal organization in France, however, is big enough, strong enough, or influential enough to constitute a real threat to the French government. And I'll stop right there!

---

1 *"À Nice, faux bus mais vrai escroc,"* Le Dauphine, March 16, 2016, www.ledauphine.com/france -monde/2016/03/16/a-nice-faux-bus-mais-vrai-escroc.
2 Laurent Borredon and Simon Piel, *"Gangs des cités ou d'Europe de l'Est: le nouveau visage du crime organisé,"* Le Monde, December 13, 2014, www.lemonde.fr/societe/article/2013/12/14/en-france -des-organisations-criminelles-mondialisees_4334429_3224.html.

Useful tip: If you're a woman, you will have significant leeway when interacting with French police officers. (But you knew that already, didn't you?)

Sound like a French person: *"Ce qui est trop marrant quand tu arrives aux États-Unis, c'est qu'il y a une ligne jaune sur le sol au bout de la queue, et personne ne bouge ou ne passe la ligne jaune. Ils sont hyper disciplinés, les gens. Je te laisse imaginer la différence avec la France . . ."* (It's too funny when you arrive in the U.S. There's this yellow line on the ground at the front of the line. Nobody budges. They just won't cross the line. People are extremely disciplined—very different from here!)

THE BOURGEOIS OBSESSION

oday's France is deeply marked both by the myth of the French Revolution and by the precepts of Marxist ideology. As such, the word *bourgeois* is incredibly common on Gallic soil.

The term *bourgeois* first appeared in medieval France: *le bourgeois* was the inhabitant of the *bourg*, frequently a shop owner. In that, he belonged to a new, forming intermediary class between the peasant and the aristocrat. As the power, wealth, and control of the aristocracy were depleted, the bourgeois grew more industrious, more influential, and richer.

After the French Revolution, different sorts of bourgeois appeared. A stratification between *petite* (artisans, shop owners), *moyenne* (doctors, lawyers, architects), and *grande* (industrialists making cultural contributions) *bourgeoisie* started to characterize French society. That's when Karl Marx and Friedrich Engels took the word *bourgeoisie* and used it to refer to the class of people who own the means of production. The bourgeois own capital while the proletariat only own their own workforce.

Bourgeois is therefore doubly negative in France—in sum, the *bourgeois* is viewed more or less as a nobility-deprived exploiter. Right-wing people will focus on the nobility-deprived side of the equation, while left-wing people will obsess over the exploiter aspect of things. Bottom line is: you don't want to be identified as a *bourgeois* in France. Several common phrases exemplify this phenomenon:

- *La mentalité bourgeoise* is a defining cornerstone of French ideology. It refers to the assumed closed-minded, unambitious, and shortsighted ways of a class that puts its own interests and its own property first.

- The figure of the *petit bourgeois* embodies this *mentalité bourgeoise*. For centuries, he's been mocked and despised for his materialistic, banal, and conformist ways.

- *Le bourgeois de province* is the bourgeois who doesn't live in Paris. His quality of life is generally superior and his name or title resonates locally. The local ecosystem comes with perks but also with drawbacks, which make some of their youth leave town and go explore.

- *S'embourgeoiser* (to become bourgeois) is the verb to describe the phenomenon that occurs as one gets older and more prosperous. Starting to like and indulge in nicer things is thus called *embourgeoisement*. It is a key term to know, as it is also used to refer to the tendency Frenchmen have to grow a little belly as they get older. Friends will approach them, tap gently on their tummies, and go: *"Eh bas, dis donc, tu t'embourgeoises . . ."* (Well, look at you. You're going all bourgeois!)

- *Bourge* is a commonly used abbreviation to refer to members of the more affluent class. It can be used as both a masculine and feminine noun (*Pierre, c'est un bourge, mais Léa, c'est vraiment une bourge*—Pierre is a *bourge*, but Léa truly is a *bourge*) or as an adjective similar to the English "bougie" (*Je suis allé à un mariage hyper bourge*—I went to this super-bougie wedding). In France, anything can be called *bourge*: a piece of clothing, a house, a first name, a school, a city, a type of cuisine, a sport . . . heck, for all you know, you are probably a *bourge*.

That is, however, unlikely. Simply because the concept of *bourgeois* seems to disintegrate when it crosses the French border. There, all of a sudden, the same mentality, traits, or drawbacks gain a form of miraculous glow. They lose their infamous social taint. Rich or industrious people overseas are surely far better than those lousy *sales bourges* over in France.

The unpopularity of the bourgeois figure led to the appearance of its newest avatar: a reinvented bourgeois . . . a *bourgeois bohème,* or *bobo* for short. The *bobo,* who passionately loves all traditional cultures and humble peoples (except for those of France, which he mocks and despises), is universally hated throughout France, probably even more so than the preceding incarnations of the bourgeois class. *Bobos,* to the rest of the country, stand for a tepid duplicity, relentless conformism, and pseudo-moral and -cultural superiority. They all flock to Paris to the point of making good old Parisian bourgeois want to leave their native city.

Ultimately, no matter what a French person is, does, or has, there will always be someone to call him a *bourgeois.* For in the end, mild acrimony is a French delicacy: French people individually and collectively just love to feed off the soft, delicious resentment fueled by the mythology associated with blurry and dated social constructs.

Useful tip: The phrase *cuisine bourgeoise* curiously has a positive connotation to it.

Sound like a French person: *"C'était hyper bourgeois, hyper guindé."* (It was super bourgeois, super stuck-up.)

L'ENA

❧

$\mathcal{I}$n 1945, the École Nationale d'Administration (ENA) was created with the objective to recruit and train executives for the French public sector—that is, what are called *les hauts fonctionnaires* (literally, "high civil servants").

What exactly is an *haut fonctionnaire*? A person with an executive position in one of the million layers of the French bureaucratic system. Think head of some ministry, key executive in some government agency, chief of staff for a minister or a mayor, ambassador, prefect, etc. The graduates from ENA are so ever present at the higher echelons of French public governance that they are known as *les énarques* (ENA grads). Monarchy is dead—énarchy is going strong! In short, while presidents, prime ministers, and ministers get replaced every so often, *les énarques* don't. And as civil servants, lifelong employment is guaranteed.

Other countries have government schools. Yet very few of these schools manage to relentlessly train individuals whose collective professional accomplishments are consistently viewed as so epically dismal to an entire country of people. It is an understatement to say that the people in charge of running the show in the French bureaucracy over the past decades have overall been doing a job so terrible that it borders on artistic performance.

Some figures for 2015:

- In France, public spending accounts for 57 percent of the country's GDP.[1]
- Poverty impacts more than five million people (making less than 50 percent of the median income) in France.
- France's debt amounted to €2.1 trillion.[2]
- The yearly trade deficit exceeded €40 billion.
- Each day, more than 170 French companies go out of business.[3]

With such results, some voices understandably criticize *les énarques* and their disconnection from the most basic principles pertaining to the economy and the real, big, open world we live in. This feeling is accentuated by the fact that many professional politicians (generally loathed by the public) are also *énarques*: since 1974, three French presidents, seven prime ministers, and countless ministers have been ENA grads, thus giving an impression that the country is being run to the ground by an incestuous class of disconnected people. Combine this with the advantages that often come along with the job—chauffeurs, low-rent fancy housing, generous pensions, free train rides, etc., always on the taxpayer's dime—and you get yourself a hearty slice of French resentment.

While there is no arguing about the mismanagement of the country and the level of disconnection of the people in charge of the French bureaucracy (countless politicians—and even more *énarques*—have never worked in a real company and have always lived off taxpayers' money),

---

1 Nicolas Goetzmann, *"57% du PIB de dépenses publiques: anatomie d'un record français construit sur une bulle des dépenses sociales depuis 40 ans,"* Atlantico, March 19, 2014, www.atlantico.fr/decryptage /57-pib-depenses-publiques-anatomie-record-francais-construit-bulle-depenses-sociales -depuis-40-ans-nicolas-goetzmann-1015137.html.
2 Marine Rabreau, *"La dette française à 2100 milliards: pourquoi c'est vraiment grave,"* Le Figaro, September 30, 2015, www.lefigaro.fr/economie/le-scan-eco/decryptage/2015/09/30/29002 -20150930ARTFIG00087-la-dette-francaise-a-2100-milliards-pourquoi-c-est-vraiment-grave.php.
3 Marie-Cécile Renault, *"Les faillites stagnent à un niveau élevé,"* Le Figaro, September 7, 2015, www .lefigaro.fr/conjoncture/2015/09/07/20002-20150907ARTFIG00109-les-faillites -stagnent-a-un-niveau-eleve.php.

blaming *les énarques* for France's predicament—while common among a certain French bourgeoisie—is somewhat shortsighted.

Énarques are ultimately enforcers of decisions made by others (the EU, particular governments, parliament, etc.). While their creative input and their go-to solution for most problems tend to materialize in the creation of a new tax or in a simple tax increase, there is no doubt that improving France's economic situation will require changing the profile of the shot-callers.

Useful tip: Avoid discussions about French bureaucracy with French people. Life's too short.

Sound like a French person: *"De toute façon, on est gouvernés par des énarques de merde."* (Anyhow, a bunch of lousy *énarques* are running this country.)

USING BUMPERS

 mericans traveling to France experience several culture shocks. Undoubtedly, one of the most striking and disturbing ones occurs upon witnessing French people park their cars.

In the United States, a person's car is an extension of the home, and as such is seen as being somewhat sacred. In short, don't mess with an American's car.

In France, the word "sacred" certainly does not apply to cars. In urban environments, where parking space is scarce and finding a spot often a nightmare, no one is thinking about their precious bumpers. When a spot has been identified, letting it go is a very last-resort option. Parallel parking is the norm, but scarcity might lead to some creative twists on this noble maneuver. Three scenarios might unfold at that point:

1. The parking job is executed perfectly: boring.

2. The parking job is executed well enough: "well enough" implies it's possible to identify the exact spot where you need to stop maneuvering—a feat generally achieved by gently nudging the car parked behind or in front. It goes like this: slowly . . . slowly . . . gentle bump. Yup, that's it; that's enough reversing.

Though some people might not love seeing their car being subjected to another driver's "good enough" parking job, they get over it since every single French person has used this technique in the past or uses it regularly.

3. The parking spot is a little too tight: Too tight is a no go. "A little too tight," however, means you can probably make it work. How? By gently using a part of the car whose existence Americans seem to forget: the bumper. It goes as follows: Gently reverse into the spot, do a gentle test push on the car behind. Gain a few inches in the process. Then try to get the nose of the car to fit in. Gentle, gentle, touch, get comfy, aaaand push, easy, easy, keep going, it's moving forward, looking good, all right, that's probably enough, now back it up again. The ambition is simple: getting the car in front to move forward a few inches. Then, if possible, the one behind as well.

Most witnesses will watch and enjoy the show. Some will help. While each and every panicking American within sight of the scene is already trying to call the police, rarely will French bystanders look distressed or shocked by the scene they're witnessing. The general feeling would be somewhere between amusement and interest. Some will look at the driver and hint at the fact that he's doing well, and that he can push a little harder. The question is not "Is he going to destroy the other cars?" but instead "Is he going to make it?" You know you've become a proper French person when you sympathize more with the person trying to make that tiny parking spot work than with the people parked in front of and behind him, whose cars are being pushed around.

Ultimately, bumpers have different functions on either side of the Atlantic: display area for stickers on the American side, parking job assistant in France. French people traveling to the U.S. surely enjoy the quintessentially American bumper stickers. For once, Americans seem to display less enthusiasm when it comes to the French twist on what is ultimately a very similar phenomenon: affirmation of self and cheeky social bonding though bumper personalization.

Useful tip: Try it!

Sound like a French person: "*Encore un peu, encore un peu, enc . . . arrête! C'est bon! Nickel . . .*" (Little more, little more, li . . . Stop! All set . . . Well-done!)

LES BISOUNOURS

$\mathcal{I}$n French, Care Bears are known as Les Bisounours (literally "kissy-bears"). If you aren't familiar with them, the Bisounours are adorable creatures designed to be loved by children. Think of a cuter pastel-colored version of the already eminently lovable teddy bear and give the little guy some adorable power like bringing happiness to others. In the French-language iteration of the show, Care Bears live in *le monde des Bisounours* (Care Bear World), a cushy-looking world found in the clouds. It's the ultimate feel-good cartoon. Most French people, whether or not they were children of the eighties and nineties, when the show was at peak popularity, know the Bisounours—if for no other reason than that most kids at the time had a stuffed Bisounours somewhere in their bedroom.

Recently the Bisounours made a comeback, but not in toy stores or on TV—instead, in the realm of political commentary. Leave it to the French to make a children's stuffed teddy into a political symbol.

In a country where changes are unending in terms of official policies and messaging, and where the public discourse has changed so radically toward a suspiciously official tolerance, some people's BS radar goes on high alert. They are constantly trying to root out the truth and motivations behind it all.

But for many other people, the official discourse incessantly promoting *la diversité, la tolérance, l'ouverture*—diversity, tolerance, openness—does sound great. Finally, people running the show have some heart, so long as we ignore the part about bombing other countries! No more borders in Europe, no more racism, no more hatred, no more discrimination, only tolerance. Real-life *monde des Bisounours*!

Finally, thanks to the ever-kindhearted media and politicians, France has a shot at being a country that feels all good inside—a huggable country.

The folks who take the official discourse at face value are typically referred to by those who don't as "Bisounours." Un-Bisounoursequely enough, the latter tend to call the others *fachos*, or fascists. While their detractors worry and question the phenomenon, the Bisounours celebrate whatever the government presents to them. While Bisounours call for more laws to "protect" the people, their critics wonder when the last time giving more power to any government led to great things for the people.

Just as Godwin's law states that if an online discussion goes on long enough, no matter what is being discussed, sooner or later someone will compare someone or something to Hitler or Nazism, right-wing conservatives in France are likely to call someone a Bisounours eventually.

Bisounours are typically criticized by their detractors for their *angélisme*—i.e., their blind idealism seeing only the best in people. Bisounours defend human rights—sometimes to extremes—and they want to build a more egalitarian society. In today's France, idealists and altruists abound in the public discourse, but they are typically criticized for being naive and disconnected, as if pessimism and defiance equaled realism and pragmatism. As if being a grown-up meant we had to resign ourselves to the worst. Thankfully enough, cooperation in human societies is not idealism, but a very likely outcome in most interactions where people really do want the best for their country and their people. Recent exciting social developments like the idea of a base salary for all or the surge of community-supported agriculture (known in France as AMAPs, or *associations pour le maintien d'une agriculture paysanne*) all show that collaboration and improvement of messed-up systems are not always unrealistic.

Useful tip: Let's all do our share to make sure our world starts resembling the Bisounours' world!

Sound like a French person: *"Alors lui, c'est les Bisounours . . . Tout le monde il est beau, tout le monde il est gentil!"* (That guy's all "Welcome to the world of Care Bears . . . Everything's beautiful, everyone's nice!")

FILLES ET FILS DE

Over the past few years, French show business has become characterized by mind-boggling nepotism.

Whether in music, film, or television, French screens and airwaves seem to be invaded by *filles et fils de* . . . (daughters and sons of . . .). Celebrity opens doors, fosters deference, and now even gets passed on to the next generation ancien régime style!

What is fascinating is how widespread the phenomenon has become, in turn closing many doors to the unlucky ones not born with the right last name or connections.

Artistic talent these days in France seems to be transmissible by blood. This is all the more amusing as French entertainers are typically chief enforcers of the leftist gospel according to which equality and openness should be the norm, anyone should be given the exact same chance, social privileges should be abolished, and redistribution is a blessing for mankind . . . even as they reap all the benefits of the lopsided reality.

The well-known French *exception culturelle* according to which the rules that apply to all other industries should not apply to the ~~entertainment industry~~ world of culture (hey, this is France!) seems to work at both a macro and a micro level. The whole industry is therefore massively subsidized with public money and is now strikingly characterized by rampant nepotism. Perks of being special: your industry and your family simply don't have to be subjected to the competitive hardships endured by the rest of the general population. Needless to say, living in this comfortable parallel reality makes it much easier to advocate for perpetuating a system viewed as quite functional, fair, and prosperous. Decidedly, most seem to fail to notice that their whole life, career, industry, and family embody the exact opposite of the propaganda and pseudo moral superiority they consistently impose on the general French public.

With the acceptance and promotion of this new generation of *fils de*, the underlying message is that talent and beauty are hereditary. Watching a lot of these performers makes it rather clear how much of a fallacy that is. Back in the ancien régime, transmission of privileges was justified by the fact that it was dictated by God. Nowadays, in a secular and materialistic society, it is harder to justify that stardom and talent shall be passed on by blood.

This change is one of the many reasons why so little French art and culture rise to the top. Striking beauties and talents fail to emerge when so many of the opportunities are taken not by those gifted with talent, but by those with connections.

For your own delight, here is a nonexhaustive list of *filles et fils de . . .* involved in various aspects of the French entertainment industry.

Nepotism, Anyone?

Antoine de Caunes	*Emma de Caunes*
Serge Gainsbourg	*Charlotte Gainsbourg*
Jean-Pierre Cassel	*Vincent Cassel*
Catherine Deneuve	*Chiara Mastroianni*
Richard Bohringer	*Romane Bohringer*
Claude Lelouch	*Salomé Lelouch*
Guy Béart	*Emmanuelle Béart*

Nepotism, Anyone?

Gérard Jugnot	Arthur Jugnot
Fabrice Luchini	Emma Luchini
Jacques Dutronc	Thomas Dutronc
Jane Birkin	Lou Doillon
Marlène Jobert	Eva Green
Alain Delon	Anthony Delon
Johnny Hallyday	Laura Smet
Gérard Depardieu	Julie Depardieu
Louis Chedid	M (Matthieu Chedid)
Jacques Higelin	Arthur H
Richard Berry	Marilou Berry
Jean-François Stévenin	Sagamore Stévenin
Guy Bedos	Nicolas Bedos
Myriam Boyer	Clovis Cornillac
Jean-Pierre Castaldi	Benjamin Castaldi

Useful tip: Good song by a *fils de*: *"Mama Sam"* by M.

Sound like a French person: *"C'est la fille Depardieu, elle, non?"* (She's Depardieu's daughter, isn't she?)

THE FRENCH
LANGUAGE

$\mathcal{T}$he French language is as beautiful as it is rich, precise, and demanding.

From the subtlety of its vocabulary to the gentle elegance of its floating feminine presence, the French language is a true enchantment.

While the English language transcribes the world as a given, the French language constantly offers the possibility to go beyond the obvious and reinvent the world. "You feel" in English may thus become *tu ressens* or *vous éprouvez*. Familiarity and emotions on the one side, distance and testing on the other. Opt for *vous ressentez* or *tu éprouves* and the resulting sentences will thus have to do with respectful interest or with friendly compassion. The French language, in essence, does not enunciate everything it says.

There exists an incredibly deep well of choices available to the French speaker to characterize a person or to meaningfully place a verb or an adverb in a sentence. Each interaction in French offers the possibility not only to describe and communicate, but also to interpret and build multiple layers of complexity and meaning into each phrase spoken.

A conversation between two people with a good command of French can be a marriage of gentle precision, of subtle open doors, and of polite refusals. To that extent, French was not so long ago the diplomatic language of choice par excellence.

However, over the past few decades French has been battered and bruised. First and foremost in France, where the bar has been lowered on the general level of written and spoken French. French people all love to hear their language spoken well: they can recognize it at once, and very few can resist the charms of their language when it is truly honored. Unfortunately, hearing French beautifully spoken has become a rare treat. Politicians and journalists with a beautiful command of French are nowhere to be found. Since the seventies, the language has slowly become simplified, bastardized . . . Consequently, many young French grow up oblivious to the beauty, the charm, and the power of their own language.

The French elite slowly lost the command of their own language as well. Just like a beautiful tennis court abandoned for lack of players and maintenance, the French language has slowly dwindled. With no role models for proper speaking, or teaching, the general population started to use an impoverished, flattened version of French. And just like that, while it lost much of its language, France also lost its unique voice.

Overseas, English has gradually became the go-to language in diplomacy, in sports, in business, and now more and more so in French universities and schools. The language of the Anglo-American empire that the French elite have allowed to take precedence has been publicized as "cool" and advertised as necessary. Tempted by Beyoncé and inspired by Steve Jobs, most younger or urban French people now speak an impoverished French constantly sprinkled not only with English words, but with the superior promises these English words seem to contain.

In France, the beautiful French language is asphyxiated. Unfortunately, so too is the world of soft elegance and measured subtlety over which a language like French can hold dominion.

Useful tip: Go check out what your local Alliance Française has to offer!

Sound like a French person: *"Le français, c'est quand même une langue magnifique, putain!"* (Damn it, French is actually a beautiful language!)

LA BISE

$\mathcal{V}$ ery few things will confuse foreigners visiting France as much as *la bise*.

La bise—often referred to as "the double-kiss thing" by foreigners— is indeed a bewildering French specialty. It follows rules that vary based on region and social setting. However, a few guidelines should help you come across as slightly less awkward, should you find yourself surrounded with *bise*-ing Frenchies:

1. If you are a woman, the rule of thumb is that *la bise* is the norm to say your hellos and good-byes to anyone who could be mistaken for a family member, a friend, a friend of a friend, or a colleague.

2. If you are a man, the general rule is that *la bise* applies to women who fall into the above category, and a handshake will work for the men.

3. At a casual social gathering (party or dinner you've been invited to), it is normal for both men and women to *faire la bise* to women they're meeting for the first time. Man-on-man action: stick to handshakes.

4. Men *bise*-ing each other can happen. However, most likely it will not to men reading this book, as Frenchmen may kiss only other men who meet strict criteria: childhood friends, very close friends, family members, and members of their sports team (particularly common among rugby players).

5. If you are to interact with someone you've never met in a public place (restaurant, bar, club, shop), no physical contact is needed, you lucky thing.

6. Should you have a good interaction with a stranger in a public setting (good conversation at a bar, fun tutoring session, etc.), if you're a woman, you might graduate from no physical contact for hellos to *la bise* for good-byes. Typically, one of these two lines will be pronounced before the *bise* becomes a reality:

   On se fait la bise?

   or

   Bon allez, on se fait la bise!

   Either of these phrases means the person has enjoyed your company and now feels a greater connection to you and is casually validating that they're about to get closer and kiss you. Take it as a ritual graduation thing: the first step toward befriending a French person. Man on man, as usual: stick to handshakes!

7. Once the *bise* has been exchanged, it is considered the new norm for this given relationship. Each French person has a precise mental database of people with whom they *font la bise* and people with whom they don't.

8. The number of *bises* depends on the region. Your best bet is to base your moves on two kisses. That will be the rule of thumb

in Paris, for instance. Travel to Montpellier, and prepare for that third one! Up to five can be acceptable in certain parts of France. On your first *bise* experience, make sure to memorize the number of *bises*, as it is most likely the one prevailing in the area. When in doubt, just consult the Web site www.CombienDe Bises.com (literally, HowManyBises.com). Yup, it is a real thing!

9. And remember, with all this *bise*-ing, form is essential. Don't be a weirdo! *Faire la bise* does not consist of kissing the other person on each cheek. That is what weird French uncles do at family gatherings. A properly executed *bise* means air-kissing when your upper cheek touches the other person's upper cheek. Be delicate.

When a French person runs into someone they haven't seen in a long time and gets a joyful and enthusiastic *bise*, this exchange typically gets recounted as follows: *Il m'a embrassé comme du bon pain!* Translation: "He kissed me like good bread!"

Surprisingly enough to many foreigners who view French people as oversexualized beasts of seduction, *la bise* does not have a sexual connotation at all! Who's the oversexualized one now . . . ?

Useful tip: While *bise*-ing, a hand on the shoulder is appropriate if you wish to convey true joy about seeing the person.

Sound like a French person: "*Ah, c'est combien ici? Trois? Quatre? Je sais jamais!*" (How many is it around here? Three? Four? I never know!)

WEALTH

Most countries in the world are home to a wealthy upper class, but in recent years France has ceased to be such a country. One simple word can explain this phenomenon: taxes.

Four decades of rampant socialism have led to the French tax man either capturing or chasing away most of the wealth created in the country.

Very few Westerners can understand the depth, the amplitude, and the consequences of the phenomenon at hand in France.

Saying that the French tax man is greedy is a gross understatement. For the richer class of French people, the level of contribution paid through taxes slowly ceased to be viewed as fair. Consequently, they started to leave the country, taking their wealth with them.

That was step one of the bleeding: rich families leaving the country.

After targeting people with cash and assets, the French government started to target people about to cash in on years of hard work: entrepreneurs. By choosing to apply an additional tax for entrepreneurs selling their businesses, they triggered a massive emigration (to Belgium, mostly) of successful entrepreneurs willing to sell their businesses without having to be up-charged for the umpteenth time by the government.

Step two of the bleeding: hardworking, creative, successful (and newly rich) entrepreneurs—gone.

But driving rich people out is not enough. A perfect socialist society cannot be complete without making it extremely difficult to become wealthy to begin with. The solution? You guessed it: taxes. High taxation of anyone educated or hardworking (or stupid) enough to be in a position to create significant value sealed the deal by progressively making it very difficult to accumulate real wealth in France. In short: try to create value in France and most of it will be captured before you get to enjoy it.

The last option for a more comfortable lifestyle is to inherit assets. But then again, the French tax man awaits, ready to capture most of the value your parents or grandparents worked their whole lives to accumulate. Mom and Dad worked hard—the French tax man thanks them.

The systematic racketeering of any value creation paired with the constant emigration of hundreds of thousands of rich, creative, and hardworking French people leaves France in a very peculiar situation: a country that is rich on paper but where cash is nowhere to be found.

Useful tip: Mo' money, mo' problems!

Sound like a French person: "*L'argent ne fait pas le bonheur.*" (Money can't buy happiness.)

THE
WEIGHT MYTH

From what we've been hearing in the United States, "Frenchwomen don't get fat."

Quite the statement that is.

Now, given the numbers laid out in the coming pages concerning the amount of fast food the French people consume and their heavy Italian favorites, either Frenchwomen are genetic freaks or we might have ourselves a bit of an urban legend here. Looking into numbers reveals that nutrition and genetics are boringly unsurprising.

Between 1997 and 2009, obesity nearly doubled in France. And if I were naughty, I would stress that the rate is actually higher among women than men, jumping from 8.5 percent in 1997 to 16 percent in 2014.[1] In 2014, the pizza/pasta/sandwich/kebab diet left a staggering 46 percent of the French population either obese or overweight.[2] In all

1 "L'obésité dans le monde: En France," Obésité Sante, www.obesite-sante.com/comprendre_l_obesite/obesite_et_surpoids/chiffres_de_l_obesite1.shtml.
2 "Obésité en France: 46% des Français en surpoids, malgré des efforts en matière d'exercice et d'alimentation," Huffington Post, March 5, 2014, www.huffingtonpost.fr/2014/03/05/46-des-francais-sont-en-surpoids-obesite_n_4905010.html.

fairness, cheeses, charcuterie, and pastries don't help, and we all know that the French can sure hold their own in front of a cheese platter.[3]

It is now even expected that by 2020 France might catch up to the United States in terms of the percentage of its population that is obese.

While undoubtedly these new eating habits highlight drastic changes in the way the French eat, they also signal the beginning of a completely new France: one inhabited by a population that has, over the past decades, grown impoverished financially, socially, and culturally.

Useful tip: If you go for a run in France, be prepared to be considered with amusement by some passersby.

Sound like a French person: *"Pff . . . j'ai pris là, faut qu'j' fasse un peu gaffe!"* (Pff . . . I put on a little weight . . . Gotta start being a little more cautious.)

3 *"Les Français champions du monde de la consommation de fromages,"* 20 Minutes, November 16, 2014, www.20minutes.fr/insolite/1481703-20141116-francais-champions-monde-consommation -fromages.

LA POLICE

$\mathcal{I}$n France, several official groups are in charge of peacekeeping:

- *la police nationale*: active in urban environments
- *la gendarmerie*: active in rural environments
- *les polices municipales*: active within the towns that created them
- *les CRS (compagnies républicaines de sécurité)*: protest police

Overall, a vast majority of French people have a positive image of the country's peacekeeping forces.[1] Unlike their counterparts in many other countries, the French police at large are not overtly corrupt, arbitrary, or violent. French people approach law enforcement officers without fear of dishonesty or brutality.

When it comes to law enforcement in France, the uneasiness is primarily felt within the ranks of law enforcement. While French society is becoming more violent (as in many other countries), French police officers are, as a group, particularly depressed. One of the main

---

1 Armel Mehani, *"Police-gendarmerie: l'éternelle querelle des frères ennemis,"* Le Point, October 24, 2014, www.lepoint.fr/societe/police-gendarmerie-l-eternelle-querelle-des-freres-ennemis-24-10-2014 -1875242_23.php.

causes for this change is the growing disconnect between the police and the judicial system. In short, police officers understandably bemoan the clemency of French courts. In France, it is possible for a police officer to arrest the same individual several times in one month, for that person to insult the officers, and yet for that person to be released every time without serious sanctions.[2] With mild impunity becoming the law of the land, policing the streets does seem to lose much of its meaning.

On the other hand, while police officers see that their actions against criminals are being undermined by overly lenient courts, they are being asked to harass and fine law-abiding citizens on the roads.

Ultimately, police officers are the first witnesses of the degradation of the social fabric. Most feel stressed and tired, many to a tragic degree: in France, a police officer is five times more likely to die of suicide than from being killed in action.[3]

This phenomenon highlights the fact that, while France surely has become a more violent society, most of the violence imposed on the French police is not physical, but psychological.

While in the United States many people fear the police, in France the reality is the exact opposite: outside the annoying speeding fines, very few people actually fear the police, particularly criminals who have grown to learn that their unlawful actions will typically go vastly unpunished. At the end of the day, French police officers suffer from their work not being valued.

Given that their missions consist of enforcing the frequently iniquitous rules dictated by a power most French people have grown to despise and view as illegitimate, it does make sense that pride and a

---

2 "Le malaise des policiers," FranceTVInfo, October 14, 2015, www.francetvinfo.fr/societe/manifes tation-des-policiers/le-malaise-des-policiers_1127579.html.
3 Flore Thomasset, "Une vaste étude confirme le malaise de la police," La Croix, March 31, 2015, www .la-croix.com/Actualite/France/Une-vaste-etude-confirme-le-malaise-de-la-police -2015-03-31-1297330.
Aziz Zemouri, "Malaise dans la police," Le Point, May 8, 2015, www.lepoint.fr/societe/malaise -dans-la-police-08-05-2015-1927240_23.php.

sense of importance in the world may not be a French police officer's bread and butter.

Useful tip: Things are not as likely to escalate with French police officers as they are in the United States.

Sound like a French person: *"Regarde moi ces cons de flics, ils en foutent pas une!"* (Look at these idiot cops. Always slacking off, aren't they?)

ENGLISH WORDS
ON T-SHIRTS

*P*assing as a French person is easy: just wear a T-shirt with an English word or two emblazoned across the chest.

Needless to say, specific words will convey a specific message about who the wearer is deep inside, but there are a few main categories into which these T-shirts tend to fall:

OPTION 1: TEES BEARING THE NAME
OF AN AMERICAN TOWN OR STATE

This is your typical gift from the uninspired mother or wife. Meeting a Frenchman with a T-shirt that says Boston, Chicago, Indiana, Baltimore, or California is simply a testament that a Frenchwoman loves him.

These T-shirts are usually sprinkled with an extra mention—also in English—that passes to the French gift giver as a sign of genuine American authenticity: "Sacramento, Since 1925." Bingo! "Nevada, Original Trademark." The extra mention does not need to make any sense in proper English. Shirts that say things like "Philadelphia—Vintage Authentic Flight Action" or "Jacksonville—Force Size Official Republic" are everywhere.

It is of paramount importance to realize that the wearer has no knowledge of what that actual city or state is like. No one is claiming anything here. The piece of clothing will always be referred to by the name of the location, pronounced with the Frenchest of accents:

T'as pas vu mon T-shirt Florida? (Have you seen my Florida T-shirt?)

OPTION 2: TEES WITH A MESSAGE

These tees appeal to a different category of French people—starting with young Frenchwomen.

Profound messages like "Fashion Victim," "I Love to Dance," or "Beautiful Vintage" flourish on French girls' clothes. The lower-class the wearer, the closer you are to a fantastically wrong statement or an act of glorious treason against the English language: "What doesn't killed me make me stronger," "Ocean, Bitch and Sunshine" . . .

As usual, hipsters break the mold in a spectacular manner: no more of that silly city thing or empty-message idiocy. Hipsters are above that. Instead, they'll sport T-shirts stating things like "Williamsburg" or "Dance till You Drop" or of course my personal favorite, "Be Different." French hipsters obviously command the delicate art of irony.

Useful tip: Relax—French people are not that classy!

Sound like a French person: *"J'sais pas trop ce que ça veut dire, mais c'est classe, c'est stylé . . ."* (Not really sure what it means, but it sure is stylish . . .)

FRENCH COMMENTS SECTIONS

The surest way to fall out of love with French people is to read the comments section of any French Web site. There, you can fathom the abyss of negativity that the average French soul has grown to harbor.

Each category of Web site displays its very own form of French negativity.

Sports sites specialize in French athlete bashing and proud *défaitisme*. A French tennis player has just won a game: comments will generally state either that he will lose the next round—guaranteed—or that the win was lucky because the other player was having a bad day. If one commenter happens to post an encouraging comment, several others will typically respond with a comment belittling that win or putting that victory in perspective with the career of Roger Federer or Rafael Nadal. It is generally understood that all French athletes and teams are terrible. It is of paramount importance to repeat it in every comment. Empty criticism shall remain the law of the comments land (the terrific neologism *rageux* applies to those practicing constant and blind criticism).

If facts are stubborn and one rare French athlete or team is successful, comments will stress that they are probably tax dodging, doped, or overpaid. In short, a successful French athlete is not a good French person.

Comments on political or news Web sites offer another interesting—but less specifically French—spectacle: people taking the bait presented to them by corporate media. Frustration and rage galore. Any dissenting opinion will either be "moderated" (read: deleted—usually by underpaid employees working for "moderation" companies in French-speaking third-world countries) or vigorously punished by other commenters.

The comments sections of open sites like YouTube are probably the most interesting in that they offer no real moderation. There, one can see the abysmally low standards of the everyday commenter. Offensive spelling, tragically mediocre command of the French language, and the reasoning capabilities of a shrimp, combined with the aggressiveness of an obnoxious small dog, are the norm. These sections will leave you somewhere between mildly heartbroken for all this sad humanity and worried for the future of France.

The only positive aspect of these black holes of negativity is that they will make any foreigner feel better about both their own country and their own command of the French language.

Useful tip: Skip them!

Sound like a French person: *"Quand tu lis les commentaires, tu sens que les gens en ont vraiment marre!"* (When you read the comments, you can tell people are really fed up!)

THE UPS AND DOWN
OF WINE CULTURE

With friends like the French government, wine culture surely doesn't need enemies. French authorities for the past decades have indeed been championing an antiwine campaign that is just as fierce as it is incongruous.

Since the early 1990s, it has been illegal to advertise wine through most main media channels in France. In those where it remains possible, no reference may ever be made to the fun or pleasure associated with wine drinking. Any time wine is to be mentioned publicly, the person talking is to remind everyone, *"L'abus d'alcool est dangereux pour la santé"* (Too much alcohol is dangerous for your health). Since then, the antiwine lobby has picked up more speed. Over the past decade alone, its track record speaks for itself: strong lobbying against online advertising for wine, full-on abstinence recommended to "combat alcoholism,"[1] studies and reports fed to the press, wine presented as

---

1 *"Le Directeur Général de la Santé prône l'abstinence et la taxation de l'alcool,"* Vitisphere, October 16, 2006, www.vitisphere.com/index.php?mode=breve&id=52272&print=1; recommendation from Directeur Général de la Santé Didier Houssin in 2006.

carcinogenic from the very first glass,[2] and a pregnant-woman logo imposed on every French wine label.

What's even more frustrating is that the statistics issued by the very official and very public INSEE on French wine consumption do not take into account tourists, who buy and drink wine during their holidays in France (that is eighty million people every year vs. sixty-five million French people) and inhabitants of bordering countries who cross the border just to fill up their trunks with wine (English, Belgians, German, Luxembourgers, Swiss, etc.). A direct consequence, of course, is that the official figures become artificially inflated and make the French seem like they drink much more wine than they actually do.

The brilliant logic that compels the French government to fight an industry that generates over a billion euros a year in taxes, plus even more less direct, but no less quantifiable, benefits in terms of image, tourism, employment, and exports is rather obvious. The French government, never short of bold ideas to plunge the country into more distress, naturally chose to become the champion of the antiwine movement. Successfully so. In France, since the 1970s, both wine consumption per capita and the number of wineries have more than halved.[3]

Here are five wine facts you'd never suspect about France:

1. Percentage of Frenchwomen who never drink wine:
   45 percent.[4]
2. Percentage of the French population who drink wine every
   day or almost every day: 21 percent.[5]

---

2 Sandrine Blanchard, *Le vin est un alcool, donc cancérigène, Le Monde,* August 2, 2009, www .lemonde.fr/vous/article/2009/08/02/dominique-maraninchi-le-vin-est-un-alcool-donc -cancerigene_1178727_3238.html.

3 *"France: La consommation d'alcool n'a jamais été aussi faible,"* iDealWine, April 15, 2014, www.ide alwine.net/2014/04/15/france-consommation-dalcool-na-jamais-ete-faible/.

"La concentration des exploitations viticoles se poursuit," Plein Champ, April 11, 2011, www.pleinchamp .com/viticulture/actualites/la-concentration-des-exploitations-viticoles-se-poursuit.

4 *"ONIVINS No.119—Étude: Les femmes et le vin,"* p. 9.

5 *"ONIVINS-INRA—La consommation de vin en France en 2005."*

3. Average budget spent on a bottle of red wine in France: three euros.[6]
4. Percentage of still wines bought in France for less than six euros per liter: 91 percent.[7]
5. Younger French consume three times less wine than their elders.[8]

Ironically enough, one thing the French government did not foresee was that, as French young people are influenced by America and American youth culture, a new American habit is slowly starting to become more hip in Gallic land: wine drinking. Consequently, on Parisian *terrasses* these days, though most clients may be drinking coffee or beer, you will find two categories of people drinking wine: Americans trying to act French, and French trying to act American.

Useful tip: Recommended read if you're interested in learning more about wine: *Into Wine* by yours truly.

Sound like a French person: *"Moi, j'achète un excellent Gaillac à €3.50, j'peux te dire qu'il fait le boulot."* (I buy an excellent Gaillac for €3.50. Let me tell you, it does the trick.)

6 *"Étude FranceAgriMer—Les achats de vins tranquilles par les ménages français pour leur consommation à domicile—Bilan annuel 2010."*
7 *"ONIVINS-INRA—La consommation de vin en France en 2005."*
8 *"ONIVINS-INRA—La consommation de vin en France en 2005"; "Les jeunes et le vin: mieux vaut prévenir,"* Vin et Société, December 10, 2010, www.vinetsociete.fr/magazine/article/les-jeunes-et-le-vin-mieux-vaut-prevenir.

LA BIEN-PENSANCE
(FRENCH P.C.)

$\mathcal{T}$wenty years back, it was customary for the French to mock America's political correctness: *"Mais les Américains, ils sont politiquement corrects."* Oh . . . the sweet feeling of intellectual superiority. Twenty years later, it is safe to say that France has caught up with the United States.

While for most French people the phrase *politiquement correct* still remains primarily associated with the U.S., France has developed two phrases of its own to refer to the French manifestation of the phenomenon:

- *la bien-pensance*: literally, "the well thinking"
- *la pensée unique*: literally, "the only way of thinking"

It is interesting to notice that the French language stresses that the limitations imposed by this new ideology are not related to the language as much as they are to the thinking. However, don't let that linguistic cuteness fool you: the speaking too shall be muzzled.

La bien-pensance establishes that one's actions, words, or reasonings should not be clogged by reality. In place of reality, there is the official narrative. Actions, words, and justifications should have no other basis than the official narrative. All observations and facts that contradict it are dangerous seeds that will lead to the rebirth of Nazism.

In short, if you disagree with the official narrative in France, you are either a Nazi or well on your way to becoming one. Your pick.

Never short of a contradiction, *les bien-pensants* like to take the moral high ground. What is true matters far less than what is (presented as) good. Truth and common sense in France have thus become suspicious. More or less obliviously so, *bien-pensants* seek to impose and legitimize a repressive, Big Brother–ish, metacommunist society[1] in which citizens all think and act uniformly, within the ever-thinning path allowed by the proponents of political correctness.

While French people generally consider *la pensée unique* as contemptible, most have to cope with their daily dose of it distilled generously through the media. Journalists are viewed as the main proponents of this ideology and widely despised for it.

Surely, daily exposure is pervasive, and as much as some French still claim to want to oppose *la pensée unique*, they ultimately internalize most of its views. This is particularly noticeable among a certain younger generation of French people who hardly know any better.

Like a dying animal on its last breath, freedom of speech and freedom of thought sometimes cause people to launch into the occasional diatribe against *le terrorisme intellectuel* (intellectual terrorism), *l'Inquisition* (the Inquisition), or *la guerre contre la réalité* (the war against reality). While others in attendance will agree to an extent with the person making such statements, they will secretly view the person voicing these opinions as a potential extremist.

The ever pervasive and ever-pernicious *bien-pensance* has slowly shaped a new society in which words and thoughts are suppressed from within.

However, some choose to resist: resistance leads to being politically incorrect—it almost requires it. Political incorrectness is therefore not

---

1 The Frankfurt School, where political correctness originates from, was Marxist in essence.

merely the silly provocation it is presented to be. It is actual dissidence. It is peaceful noncompliance.

But ultimately, today's France struggles with dissenting voices. The French regime fights hard to condemn dissidents by any means possible. From passing laws of exception that criminalize questioning official history—like the Gayssot Act, which makes it illegal to question the war crimes prosecuted in the Nuremberg Tribunal (a law Noam Chomsky himself disavowed)[2]—to Soviet-like attempts to harrass politically incorrect intellectuals, comedians, or even children,[3] today's France sure starts to resemble the brave new society, devoid of deviant thinking, the proponents of *bien-pensance* hope to establish.

Try to mention that this new France has every characteristic of a tyrannical regime and . . . surprise, surprise . . . you'll be pinned as a Nazi extremist!

Useful French adjective for you these days: *Orwellien!*

Useful tip: Resist!

Sound like a French person: *"On peut plus rien dire, c'est dingue!"* (It's nuts. You just gotta keep your mouth shut these days!)

---

2 Noam Chomsky, *"Contre la loi Gayssot,"* September 5, 2010, www.noam-chomsky.fr/contre-la-loi-gayssot/.

3 Matthieu Suc and Eric Nunès, *"Apologie du terrorisme: pourquoi un enfant de 8 ans a-t-il été entendu,"* *Le Monde,* January 29, 2015, www.lemonde.fr/les-decodeurs/article/2015/01/29/apologie-du-terrorisme-pourquoi-un-enfant-de-8-ans-a-t-il-ete-entendu-par-la-police_4566129_4355770.html. *"France: Un troisième enfant musulman interrogé par la police pour 'apologie du terrorisme,'"* *Alter Info,* February 3, 2015, www.alterinfo.net/notes/France-Un-troisieme-enfant-musulman-interroge-par-la-police-pour-apologie-du-terrorisme_b7424180.html.

YOGURT

*P*eople think of France as the country of cheese. Really, it's the country of yogurt.

Indeed, yogurt has become a consistent landmark in every boring French meal. As much as foreigners like to imagine the French feasting on delicious home-cooked meals all day, every day, realistically, in France like anywhere else, your typical eating day resembles the following: sleepy breakfast, speedy lunch at work, and tired dinner with the kids.

In all three instances, yogurt might pop up on the table. There is no guarantee of a yogurt-free meal in France. It simply does not exist. With French parents usually insisting on their children having at least one form of *laitage* (dairy product) per meal, you know you're in for some cheese or yogurt.

Consequently, while your typical American family always has pickles and ketchup in the fridge, your typical French fridge is always home to some supermarket cheese and a few cups of yogurt. Just in case.

The quality and variety of yogurt in France is rather high. Some yogurt is deemed healthy and light; some is so delicious you know it's actually dessert (Danette, anyone?). Some types have *morceaux* (fruit chunks); some don't. The *yaourt nature* (plain yogurt) is a beautiful classic: before you eat it, you get to add powdered sugar. You know you're having a sophisticated meal when the brick of powdered sugar ends up on the dinner table. Try to play it cool and not add sugar to your *yaourt nature?* You will most likely regret it.

Yogurt in France is brought to the table right after the main course as a guilt-free transition or an alternative to a light dessert. At home, the meal rarely ends with crème brûlée, profiteroles, or chocolate mousse: a cup of yogurt and a piece of fruit is the real unspoken ticket to Frenchness.

Useful tip: Venture out and try delicious *fromage blanc*—a great alternative to yogurt.

Sound like a French person: "*Yaourt: avec ou sans morceaux?*" (Yogurt: with or without fruit chunks?)

STRIKES

*A*cross the globe, countless people view the French as always being on strike, which is unfair. Sometimes, they are on vacation.

When it comes to the delicate art of striking, though not enough comprehensive data exists to give the French a solid gold medal outright, it is fair to assess that France is definitely one of the leading nations in the world.

Worldwide, liberals will admire the French while conservatives will mock them for it. However, what most fail to notice is that there is a key difference to acknowledge: whether the strike—*la grève*—involves the public or the private sector. While employees in the private sector hardly ever strike, the French public sector is home to the very best strikers on the planet. No question about it: the Michael Jordans and Tiger Woodses of strikes all can be found in the French public sector.

If you have been to France, you have most likely experienced at least one such strike: Paris metro staff, airport workers, bus drivers, Air France pilots . . . these are as recurring as they are unpleasant. Horror stories of students missing exams or of small companies being run to the ground due to the consequences of a prolonged strike add to the more banal horrors: countless hours of waiting, packed (and smelly) metros, horrid traffic, and frustration all around.

The French who get caught up in the chaotic consequences of public workers' strikes like to say that they are *pris en otage* (taken hostage). Unions don't shy away from using strikes during peak times that will create the highest amount of disruption and thus give them (they think) the greatest leverage. There's even a term for this strategy: *la grève ciblée* (targeted strike). Typical examples: airport workers going on strike when most French people intend to vacation or, even better, Air France pilots going on strike just as the soccer World Cup was about to start in France.

While some still support strikers, a growing number of French people have grown quite aggravated by what they deem an excessive usage of their *capacité de nuisance*. It should be noted that strikes of a new kind have recently started to appear in the metro and bus systems: strikes due to physical violence (muggings, beatings) suffered by agents. In solidarity and as a call to action for management, drivers will stop working for a day or two.

All in all, getting a bike is probably a good idea!

Useful tip: Strikes are more successful when the weather is nice. If it rains, chances are disruptions will be minor. If forecasts announce sunshine, your best bet is to plan a picnic in the park!

Sound like a French person: *"Fais gaffe, ils annoncent une grève mardi."* (Watch out. There's supposed to be a strike on Tuesday.)

TELEVISED DEBATES

❧

French television specializes in placing suit-wearing people in front of a camera and having them speak over one another.

That, to the French, is an exhilarating spectacle. After all, good entertainment surely can consist of watching beautifully prepared professionals perform live in a discipline that they certainly enjoy and indeed—don't make me blush—dabble with occasionally and derive pleasure from in their free time. This in France applies to sports, of course, and to debating about politics. When it comes to entertainment, an evening spent watching politicians talk on TV is plenty good for most French people. Not that debates are typically as entertaining as a good sports game, but they do satisfy that strange side of the French brain that derives a significant amount of pleasure from talking about politics and assembling the argumentative blocks that will lead to the delightfully rational crushing defeat of the people you disagree with (because, let's face it, any hope of convincing them would be illusory). Talking about politics in France is a sport. Make debating policies an Olympic event and watch France become the nation to beat!

While most other countries have occasional televised exchanges between pundits on given topics, they tend to limit these interactions to less than five minutes: "John, Jerry, thank you for your input, gentlemen. Have a great day."

Rookies.

To the French, a five-minute interaction does not even qualify as an interaction—merely an *amuse-bouche*. A thirty-minute televised discussion is acceptable, but realistically the meat can really only be found in a good old two-hour prime-time debate show.

The recipe for a good French *débat*? Inviting guests expected to voice noncommittal thoughts and opinions on a vague topic and have a neutral journalist moderate the exchange.

If you were French, that last sentence would have triggered a mild thrill of excitement down your spine . . .

For a successful show, it is of paramount importance to respect a few rules:

1. No progress should ever be made: a constructive political discussion is simply not a thing in France.
2. People who deem it relevant to question the foundations or the legitimacy of an established system are not welcome guests.
3. It is fully acceptable to interrupt or speak over other guests at length.
4. Guests should primarily be politicians: as a general rule, people not living off taxpayers' money are simply not as worthy to discuss anything at all.

Secretly, French viewers hope for things to escalate. While insults are a lovely thing to hope for, the real juicy part of a good TV debate is for one guest to leave the set outraged. That will plunge the French watcher into a mildly perverse joy. The incident will be discussed at work the next day and the influx of palpable testosterone will take weeks to be fully digested. Guilty rewatches on YouTube will occur for the more technology savvy.

France's hypnotic addiction to *les débats* is such that you'll find them on most channels, most days, at all times of the day. A foreigner turning on the TV in France will grow incredulous:

Man, look at these guys. They go on and on—it's nuts . . . What are they even talking about?

Soon enough, the zoo syndrome will inevitably settle in:

Look at that one with the blue tie—gosh, he's animated, that one! Oh, and look at that lady—she looks so angry right now. It's hilarious!

Foreigners mocking their beloved *débats* is disturbing to French people. They will laugh and somehow question whether what they have always viewed as noble democracy at work might actually just be a laughable spectacle.

But ultimately their own certitudes, shaped by decades of debate watching, will not be shaken that easily: these programs are worthwhile and far superior to crass Anglo-Saxon television. *There.*

By watching people tell them what to think, French people know they are growing more informed and educated. Miraculously, from the spoon-feeding process, French people manage to derive a sense of superiority.

It takes rare psychological skills to be French.

Useful tip: Most likely, if it's on TV and it's about politics, the odds that it's worth your time are slim to none!

Sound like a French person: *"T'as vu le débat entre Marine Le Pen et Manuel Valls? C'était chaud, putain!"* (Did you see the debate between Marine Le Pen and Manuel Valls? Heated, huh?!)

BREAD

$\mathcal{M}$ost visitors arriving at a French dinner table will be faced with a small but very real challenge. The diner will see the bread basket, inevitably she will pluck out a *morceau de pain*, and . . . that is precisely when her troubles start.

For after picking it up, she'll soon enough realize that she has nowhere to put that piece of bread. The bread plate is MIA. In an attempt to stay cool and composed, most people will opt for a cheeky move: keeping the piece of bread sitting on their napkin until the first course is served. The strategy is well established: the edges of the plate in front of her will make for a safe haven for the bread. With confidence in that strategy, the foreign diner will regain her original tranquillity.

But when the plate does arrive, the diner realizes with horror that the edges are not flat. Still, she will position the bread there. Only to find out that, with a disappointing obedience to the basic rules of physics, the piece of bread will start sliding down . . . straight into the food. Frustration, embarrassment, and discreet gluttony typically ensue.

The French way to solve this apparently unsolvable equation is simple: just put the bread on the table.

It is utterly irrelevant to the French whether the table is covered with a tablecloth or whether the surface on which the bread will be placed has any semblance of cleanliness. On the table is simply where your piece of bread belongs. More precisely, and according to French etiquette, on the top left corner of your place setting is where your piece of bread belongs.

If you like bread and find yourself in France, it is essential to let go of the modern obsession with bacteria and cleanliness. If you're worried about these, just drink wine! That'll take care of it!

A similar situation is bound to vex a foreign visitor at the bakery: the *vendeuse* will almost certainly pick the bread she will hand you with her bare hands. Most French people would almost feel offended if she did not. Heck, the good client at a bakery is easy to spot: it's that person the *vendeuse* will go out of her way for, feeling up five to ten different baguettes to pick the perfect one for that special shopper. Oh, the delights of this very French moment where discreet sensuality and outstanding customer service become one.

In France, bread is so intrinsically part of everyday life that the relationship to it is entirely carnal. Bread is an extension of the French body and an expression of its undying soul. Each day, in hundreds of sushi or Chinese restaurants, you will find French patrons asking for some bread, for no matter how ricey your meal is, it's still a meal and therefore calls for some bread. The ominous American threat known as "carbicide" is one that has never crossed any French person's thoughts. Ever. And truthfully, if they were familiar with the term, most French people would simply order more bread, just to make a point.

Useful tip: Try *une baguette tradition* (aka *une tradi*) over the simple baguette.

Sound like a French person: *"Théo, tu peux aller chercher le pain, s'il te plaît?"* (Théo, can you please go get the bread?)

LES FONCTIONNAIRES

The French state is one far-reaching octopus. Anyone who gets paid by an entity controlled by the French state is referred to as a *fonctionnaire*. A *fonctionnaire* can be a teacher, a local government employee, a nurse, a train driver, a police officer, a postal worker, a tax collector, a professor, a bus driver, or a bureaucrat of really any sort . . .

Fonctionnaires make up about 25 percent of the French labor force—that is over 5.5 million people.[1]

While many *fonctionnaires* have jobs that are not quite exhilarating, they sure come with lovely perks:

PERK 1: Eighty percent of *fonctionnaires* simply cannot be fired.[2] Mess up in epic proportions? It's okay. Lifelong employment. Who said, "What's the incentive to work, then?"? You dirty capitalist, you!

---

1 *"Les fonctionnaires sont les champions des vacances," Observatoire des Gaspillages,* July 31, 2013, www.observatoiredesgaspillages.com/2013/07/les-fonctionnaires-sont-les-champions-des-vacances/.
2 *"Les sept avantages du statut des fonctionnaires," Le Figaro,* August 31, 2012, www.lefigaro.fr/conjoncture/2012/08/31/20002-20120831ARTFIG00454-les-sept-avantages-d-un-statut-d-exception.php?pagination=2#nbcomments.

PERK 2: On average, *fonctionnaires* are paid more than private sector employees. Their wages increase faster too.

PERK 3: On average, *fonctionnaires* work fewer hours than private sector employees. They also work fewer and fewer hours.

PERK 4: *Fonctionnaires* get to call in sick (much) more than private sector employees. On average, a local government employee calls in sick a mind-blowing 22.3 days a year. Yes, that is close to one month a year. (And yes, they still get paid when they do.)

PERK 5: *Fonctionnaires* get extra cash each month when they have children.

PERK 6: Many *fonctionnaires* get to retire at age fifty-seven, some at age fifty-two.

Fonctionnaire bashing is a recurring conversation for French people employed in the private sector. Though most French people are grateful for *les services publics*, many suspect that the number of *fonctionnaires* employed to supply these services is excessive and the advantages they enjoy *scandaleux*. Altogether, many reckon that functionaries are *privilégiés*. Among these, the hundreds of thousands working vaguely useless administrative positions are dubbed *des planqués* (literally, "the ones in hiding").

As much as they like to bash them and point out their advantages, very few private sector employees would ever consider becoming a *fonctionnaire*. Apparently, the advantages do not quite compensate enough to justify the looming perspective of having to work for one of the least exciting and most overarching bureaucracies in the world.

While over the past few years all comparable countries have been cutting the number and, frequently, the advantages of their own *fonctionnaires*, France has been hiring more and more of them. With successive politicians lacking the courage to take the measures that would effectively lead to the reversal of the unemployment curve, they wisely reasoned that a great way for unemployment to go down was to hire more *fonctionnaires*.

Smart.

Most French youngsters share their government's absence of courage and general disconnection with the basic rules of the world economy we live in: 73 percent of young French people would like to become *fonctionnaires* for their careers.[3] It is reassuring to see that the vast majority of left-leaning French teachers managed not to pass their views on to their pupils.

Little do the young realize that, while working for the government is indeed safe (should one consider that working for a virtually bankrupt employer is safe), it surely is becoming less and less pleasant in a number of professions—police officers, teachers, nurses—that have to deal directly with a population that is growing more violent and less respectful by the hour. Interestingly, while historically a vast majority of *fonctionnaires* voted for the Socialist Party, the appeal of that party is eroding as more and more civil servants have to witness the mess their country is in on a daily basis.

All in all, one quarter of the French workforce works for the state. Add an odd 22 percent that is (more or less) unemployed,[4] and you realize that only half of French adults actually have a job in the private sector. It could be argued that 50 percent of the workforce is paying for the other 50 percent.[5] One France looks at the other with mild scorn and an inability to truly understand. The fiscal escalation and the general lack of perspective that this *fonctionarisation* of French society

3 "*Les 3/4 des jeunes Français rêvent de devenir fonctionnaires*," *BFMTV*, March 23, 2012, www.bfmtv.com/societe/les-3-4-des-jeunes-francais-revent-de-devenir-fonctionnaires-239891.html.

4 Marc Lassort, *France: Le vrai taux de chômage est de 21,1%*," *IREF*, June 14, 2015, http://fr.irefeurope.org/France-le-vrai-taux-de-chomage-est-de-21-1,a3388.

5 "*Plus de 50% des actifs payés par de l'argent public: le vrai poids de l'État français*," *Atlantico*, December 4, 2013, www.atlantico.fr/decryptage/plus-50-actifs-payes-argent-public-vrai-poids-etat-francais-jean-philippe-delsol-916481.html.

has incited come with a new ambition, a new hope for French people who wish to work in the private sector: leaving the country to live and work abroad.

The ultimate French move is thus to go be a *fonctionnaire* overseas! Double whammy!

Useful tip: The term *les services publics* refers to all the services rendered by *la fonction publique* (aka *les fonctionnaires*).

Sound like a French person: "*Oui, enfin, tous les fonctionnaires ne sont pas logés à la même enseigne: un prof en banlieue et un employé du conseil régional, c'est pas la même chose!*" (Okay, but not all public servants are the same: a teacher in the hood and a paper pusher in local government are two very different things.)

NICE THINGS

France has a history of being pretty good at making nice things. When it comes to architecture, fashion, food, and wine, the French are up there in the pantheon of people who have excelled at creating beauty in the world.

However, a more current look sheds a different light on the contemporary relationship between the French and nice things.

First off, while in English the adjective "nice," when applied to a building, a neighborhood, or a car immediately makes sense to all, it is not the case in French. Simply, for in French there is no direct equivalent to the word "nice" when used to describe these things.

A nice neighborhood in French is *un quartier chic* or *un beau quartier*. Both have a significant negative socialist-infused undertone. Hipsters talk about their gentrified areas as *un super quartier*, but while those neighborhoods may have character, they are not, so to speak, "nice."

The same goes in the field of new constructions. Travel to Asia, to Dubai, to Brazil, or to the United States and you'll see plenty of nice new buildings: nice airports, nice office buildings, nice houses . . . In France, while some examples do exist, you'll have to get quite lucky to find nice new things. France is mainly a country of nice old things (châteaux, cathedrals, churches, buildings, etc.)

Most recent constructions in France look and feel incidentally rather far from nice. While old-school France, with its castles, churches, cathedrals and villages, could show the world how to do nice, new-school France could learn a thing or two from other countries—but it is most likely not going to happen anytime soon. There are two reasons for that.

First, construction in France is a world where norms and regulations have become so onerous and their application so costly that creating niceness or beauty has grown to be a preoccupation that generally ranks somewhere between secondary and unrealistic.

Most people don't aspire to nice. They aspire to good enough. They don't hope for beautiful; they yearn for safe. The triumph of relativism has led to a constant undermining of the notion of beauty itself. Most French these days would argue that beauty is a personal construct. Argue that it is rare for a human not to find a sunset beautiful and you will be classified as a fascist. If beauty is no longer a thing, ugliness can't be either.

One of the most telling consequences of this new relationship to architecture is the terrifying spread of horrifying commercial areas that now surround every small town in France. While you'll find very few French people bold enough to call them pretty, their mere existence is a symptom of a society that no longer holds beauty in the high regard it used to.

And when it comes to nice clothes, very few French people opt for genuine quality. The success of low-quality clothing brands and concepts goes to show the interesting dichotomy of modern France. On the one hand, it is home to some of the most well-known and most successful luxury brands in the world; on the other, most French people wear clothes they buy from the H&Ms of the world.

Useful tip: Nice French wines are not necessarily expensive. Patronizing a good wine shop will help you find fantastic-value wine.

Sound like a French person: *"C'est très chicos, ça, comme quartier!"* (That's a really posh neighborhood!)

IMMIGRATION

*I*n France, like in most Western countries, the topic of immigration has been distorted in ways that would humble any Soviet propagandist. For some, the mere indication that you wish to discuss immigration will make you a racist of some sort.

However, it is key to explore the topic in order to reach a good understanding of the state of France's political situation these days. First of all, historically, until a few decades ago, immigration was indeed viewed as a sneaky move to keep salaries down and undermine the influence of trade unions. Immigration was viewed as social dumping and detrimental to the working class. As such, left-wing parties understandably opposed it fiercely.

The so-called right opened the floodgates in 1976 when *regroupement familial* was institutionalized, whereby an immigrant with a job could have his entire family join him in France. Soon after, the so-called left started to turn its back on the French working class by joining the so-called right in becoming advocates of immigration. Massive numbers of immigrants from North and sub-Saharan Africa started to come to France. No longer just men coming to work, possibly meeting a Frenchwoman, and ultimately integrating into French society, but entire families with women and children. The share of immigrants coming to work was by nature low.

It is key at this point to realize that the mid-1970s in France marked the end of the *"Trente Glorieuses"*—the three "glorious" decades of prosperity after World War II. The following four decades in France have been decades of slow economic growth and high unemployment, meaning the reason for immigration was not because France needed more workers: France already had too many workers and not enough jobs.

Despite the hardships linked to leaving one's country of origin, the generosity of the French state toward immigrants usually made it all rather worth it for them. Having a job was almost secondary, as the sum of various subsidies frequently amounted to more money at the end of the month than a small salary. Most immigrants ended up living in the same areas (the famous *banlieues*), which led them to keep their languages and traditions and not to blend into French society. The fact that these *banlieues* are probably some of the most depressing places to live on this planet did not help.

Copious amounts of propaganda were directed at all levels of French society, leading French people to accept legislation that many believed to be detrimental to them. *L'antiracisme* became one of the key battles of the French Republic. No one was to question immigration and its benefits for the country. Immigration was *"une chance pour la France."* Period. Anyone bold enough to even put that statement into question was demonized and immediately portrayed as a racist. Recently, new heights in the criminalization of dissent on the topic of immigration were reached when a retired French general—former head of the prestigious Légion Étrangère (Foreign Legion)—was arrested by the police while partaking in a peaceful rally against the settling of migrants in France.

Over the past few decades, it has been made very clear to the French that when it comes to mass immigration, they are to politely comply and get used to their country changing before their eyes.

Four decades of the setup following the passage of the pro-immigration legislation have entirely changed France. Millions of immigrants have arrived in the country; they have had children and grandchildren. The social, ethnic, religious, and cultural makeup of French society have been changed in deep, incalculable ways that are difficult to grasp.

Today, realistically, the general cultural, moral, and economic impoverishment of French society, paired with the rise of permissiveness, violence, and the rampant spread of radical Islam, attest to at least one thing: the consequences of mass immigration are questionable.

Year after year, France changes visibly: between 1999 and 2011 alone, the population of foreign descent (foreign over two generations) increased by 2.4 million to reach 12.3 million people. That is an increase rate of 25 percent. The increase rate for the rest of the French population was 4.4 percent.[1] In light of such figures, the theory of the *"grand remplacement"* comes across not as right-wing lunacy but as mere mathematical reality.

Taking a few steps back helps shed an interesting light on our Western democracies. In France, like in most Western nations, mass immigration in an era of mass unemployment is a subject on which the people were never consulted. There has never been a vote asking people whether they thought mass immigration was a good idea or whether it should be paused or slowed down at some point.

People viewing immigration as a means used by the rich and powerful to advance their interests might not have been that far off in the end!

---

1 "Michèle Tribalat: *'Les politiques sont désemparés face à l'immigration,'*" *Observatoire du Grand Remplacement*, October 16, 2014, www.grand-remplacement.com/michele-tribalat-les-politiques -sont-desempares-face-a-limmigration/.

Useful tip: The perception of immigration in France and in the U.S. is quite different. The common American view according to which "immigrants do the jobs citizens don't want to do" is not as common in Europe (where mass unemployment is more widespread and public subsidies are numerous and generous).

Sound like a French person: *"Moi, j'suis pas raciste, mais quand même . . ."* (I'm not racist, but honestly . . .)

FRENCH CARS

Though those two words put together tend to trigger hilarity in North America, there is such a thing as a French car!

France boasts three large historical car manufacturers: Renault, Peugeot, and Citroën. French engineers have accumulated tremendous know-how in the automotive field—crowned by multiple racing titles and millions of cars sold throughout the world (except in North America, where most people still have no idea the French even make cars). These three carmakers were all born in the late nineteenth century. To this day, over half the cars sold in France are produced by these three brands (controlled by two companies, as Peugeot and Citroën are now part of the same group, PSA). Many French families develop a particular relationship with and lifelong loyalty to one of the three brands.

It is fascinating to observe that the evolution of French cars follows to a T the evolution of the French people.

In the fifties, French cars were robust and stylish; in the sixties, they were powerful and imposing. Then things started to go downhill. By the nineties, mild crappiness in French cars had become the norm. Nowadays, your average French car is about as stylish as your average French person—not much.

Most French people would, of course, argue otherwise. They will argue that, for most, cars are no longer meant to display social status. True. They will tell you that big cars are not fuel efficient. Fair enough. Some will say that buying a French car means supporting domestic businesses. To an extent. They will say that a small car is easier to park and really all they need. Yup.

The adjectives commonly used to describe cars in France have thus shifted. No more *élégant* or *racé* (classy). Instead, lots of *mignon* and *chou* (cute). Today, over half the cars bought in France are *citadines*—i.e., small cars designed for short rides and city dwelling. Cuteness galore on French roads indeed.

Some would argue that such a trend reflects a form of pauperization of France. That would be only partially true, as many people who could afford nicer cars simply choose not to buy them. All the more so as the social stigma of driving a big—or nice—car in France has become quite sharp: you will be identified as *un gros con* (a big jerk) or *un gros riche* (a rich hotshot) by a number of people. For the more brainwashed of French leftists, it's a double combo: drive a nice car and you'll be *un gros con de riche*. Not only is driving a nice car more expensive; it's also a subversive social statement in France. No wonder numbers are dropping!

A broader analysis would lead one to look into the mental evolution at play here: while a few decades ago words like "panache," "elegance," and "boldness" were cardinal values of the French identity, they have grown to lose their appeal for most French people. Words like "value," "cuteness," and "convenience" seem to strike more of a chord in France these days.

In cars, as with most other things, dissenting by aiming high has become suspicious. Conforming by aiming low, however, has become the norm. If the reputation of the French manufacturers overseas is anything to go by,[1] it seems that this makes the French a rather unique people!

---

1 Alain-Gabriel Verdevoye, *"Les automobiles françaises n'ont pas la cote à l'étranger,"* *Challenges*, April 3, 2015, www.challenges.fr/entreprise/20150402.CHA4562/les-automobiles-francaises-n-ont -pas-la-cote-a-l-etranger.html.

Useful tip: Should you drive through the small villages of France, sometimes a small French car might prove far more convenient than a big non-French car!

Sound like a French person: *"Je roule français, moi, monsieur!"* (I drive a French car, sir!) A semi-ironic line, typically.

THE RISE OF
COMMUNITIES

$\mathcal{T}$he French Republic recognizes no intermediary between the individual and the state. Legal tradition establishes that, no matter your origin, your creed, or the color of your skin, if you are French, you are first and foremost a French citizen. You are not primarily Christian, black, Corsican, Muslim, blind, homosexual, or into golf. You are French.

The French love to point to what they refer to as *le modèle communautariste américain*, whereby, they reckon, communities coexist and compete but don't really mix. The French refusal to recognize communities responded to the ambition to assimilate and welcome all citizens into Frenchness.

Your main identifier was not your region, your religion, or your skin color, but your country. And you were not really given a choice: backtrack a few decades and you'll find very adamant French authorities deliberately obliterating regional particularisms (languages, traditions, and religious beliefs) in order to establish Frenchness everywhere in the territory, above all other forms of identity or feelings of belonging. Bretons, Basques, or Savoyards were to become French.

Though violent and deeply destructive to the cultural practices and heritage unique to certain areas of France, this process has been crowned with a great deal of success. After a period of adjustment, French people ended up becoming the notoriously—and sometimes obnoxiously—proud French we know and love today.

However, over the past decades, things have changed tremendously. The idea of one united nation ceased to be hip. With the establishment of the European Union, the mere concept of a European nation was entirely diluted by the already strong and established identities of each of the countries that joined. Consequently, the agenda of "diluting the French nation" in favor of a "European" identity begged for a change of strategy. Can't redraw the borders of nations and have people clinging to their old nation, can you?

For people living in France, the legitimate sense of belonging had to cease being Frenchness as they had previously known it. Surreptitiously, new "communities" based on ethnicity, religion, origin, gender, and sexual orientation started to become organized, promoted, funded, and publicized.

And just like that, while most French people were still making fun of *le modèle communautariste américain*, France started not only to recognize communities but also to adapt the old French political and social systems to them.

Basically, French people witnessed not only the official birth but also the rapid takeover of special interest groups. Politicians no longer had to worry about French people as one united force, but instead about socially active, and socially powerful, "communities."

In short, France entered the world of "modern democracies" in which the silent majority commonly has to bow down to the interests of the socially active minorities.

Useful tip: Just wait until the French become a "minority" in your country. Major pressure on your baking industry awaits you!

Sound like a French person: *"Ça, c'est le modèle communautariste américain, c'est pas le modèle français!"* (That's the American community-based model, not the French model!)

FRENCH UNIVERSITIES

The French university system may seem complex at first, but understanding the following elements will help you make sense of it.

All that is required to attend a French university is to graduate from high school. Enrolling is extremely inexpensive and, as a general rule, no further examination or prerequisite is needed. In that, French universities strangely resemble the military, free concerts, or really seedy bars.

Once enrolled in a French university program, students are subjected to almost unbearable pressure: to move on from year to year; the only requirement to speak of is simply to pass. Passing in France is known as *avoir la moyenne*—that is, reaching the grade of 10 out of 20. Success in French universities is quite literally reaching the average. Thus, a French student may obtain master's degrees in all sorts of subjects while having been a very mediocre student all his life. Strangely enough, the job market took notice and seems to show limited interest in profiles of people who have never been subjected to any form of competitive examination at any point during their adult lives.

France thus produces thousands of graduates each year with master's degrees in fields resulting in high employability like sociology, history, psychology, or art history. These people usually end up working for the government, unemployed or—in their view—underemployed. Most of them view themselves as *surqualifiés* (overqualified) and truly struggle to fathom why employers may opt for other graduates with professional experience, a habit of performing in a competitive environment, and an ability to anticipate what's coming and to act accordingly, rather than for their self-important selves. Employers truly are capitalist pigs.

Consequently, a vast majority of the best French students—or those coming from families with an understanding of how the job market functions—choose to study their way out of the traditional French university system. Several options for them:

- Enroll in a *formation professionnalisante* (BTS, DUT, etc.): Shorter, more hands-on vocational training resulting in more job opportunities.

- Go to private school: Pay your way into what will be viewed as an *école pour fille/fils à papa*—a school for daddy's girls and boys—but that usually (surprise, surprise) will get you a job when you graduate.

- Attend a *classe préparatoire* (aka *prépa*): Two years of very intense cramming, open only to the best students in high school, that will open the doors to highly competitive *grandes écoles* (such as business or engineering schools). Double selection process.

- *Faire médecine*: Enroll in med school, which starts at the undergraduate level; selection occurs at the end of year one.

The direct consequence of these alternatives is the gradual but constant degradation of the talent pool in the traditional university system. Thankfully, exceptions do exist, but, simply put, the best and brightest French students are rarely found in traditional French universities.

The traditional French university system is public and as such characterized by a strong disconnect with the job market and the professional world in general. This is often emphasized by rampant leftism among both students and professors. Most companies much prefer to fund, sponsor, and hire from the *grandes écoles*, which are viewed as harder to get into and more in touch with the real world. Endowment in most French universities is therefore quite low, particularly compared with U.S. universities.

While in the UK, for instance, one can become an investment banker after studying philosophy at Oxford, this does not happen in France. Academic prestige—linked both to selectivity and professional success—has deserted public universities and is now almost exclusive to the *grandes écoles*. La Sorbonne has long ceased to be a desirable line on a French person's résumé. France does not have an Oxford or a Cambridge; it does not have a Yale or a Harvard. What it has is *grandes écoles* for business (ESSEC, HEC) and others for engineering (Polytechnique, Centrale, Mines). This fragmentation makes it poorly understood by others.

The result is a divided system where, in a very French way, each side looks down on the other:

- Public university people view *grandes écoles* people as the spawn of the capitalist overlords willing to shape docile and hardworking managers.

- *Grandes écoles* people view the university types as disconnected leftists wasting public money on a strangely inflated sense of self-importance and intellectual power.

No matter what the trials and tribulations of its education system are, France will be France!

Useful tip: Great towns for an exchange program in France include Paris, Aix, Montpellier, and Rennes.

Sound like a French person: *"Les universités américaines, c'est quelque chose!"* (American universities are something else!)

LES ASSOCIATIONS

$\mathcal{J}$ust two trillion euros in debt, France obviously knows a thing or two about sound management of public money.

One of the most interesting habits the French government has developed to spend taxpayers' money (taxpayers who, interestingly enough, are termed *contribuables*) is to fund *associations*. There are 1.3 million *associations* in France, ranging from your local Scrabble club to very influential LGBT groups.

While 80 percent of French *associations* get no money at all from the government, 7 percent of them collect 70 percent of all public subsidies.

Of course it's fair.

Petty cash, you reckon? Try €34 billion a year![1] That is approximately 9 percent of the total budget of the French government. To give you an idea, that number exceeds the entirety of the budgets of countries such as Croatia, Morocco, or Nigeria.

The culture of giving away free money to certain groups—no matter how obscure they are—has grown to become an intrinsic part of

---

1 Sophie Humann, *"Ces très 'chères' associations,"* Le Figaro, June 29, 2012, www.lefigaro.fr/lefigaro magazine/2012/06/29/01006-20120629ARTFIG00476-ces-tres-cheres-associations.php.

all levels of political life in France. National, regional, local: most elected officials in France don't seem to be able to resist the irresistible urge to redistribute other people's money. Corruption is rampant in France—but, as opposed to most other countries, politicians don't only collect the checks; they also write them. (Not from their own bank accounts, though, obviously!)

The French language has come up with neat neologisms to describe this system:

- *le copinage* (from *copain*, "buddy"): "You scratch my back; I scratch yours."
- *le renvoi d'ascenseur*: Favors in return (literally, "elevator return trip").
- *la subventionnite*: The disease related to subventions (subsidies), or "subsidy-itis."

Needless to say, you are more likely to receive money if you meet certain criteria—say, if you:

- have dirt on some elected official.[2]
- represent a community you can mobilize to vote for a certain party or candidate.[3]
- work for a branch of government and use it to the advantage of your peers (and yourself).
- are related to or friends with people who allocate subsidies (and you don't mind the occasional kickback).[4]

---

2 Alain Pucciarelli, *"Marseille: subventions et copinages?," Mediapart*, April 24, 2015, https://blogs.mediapart.fr/pucciarelli-alain/blog/240415/marseille-subventions-et-copinages.

3 David Perrotin, *"Subventions: heureux comme un adjoint de Lagarde à Drancy," Rue89*, November 13, 2014, http://rue89.nouvelobs.com/2014/11/13/subventions-heureux-comme-adjoint-lagarde-a-drancy-256026.

4 Clotilde Alfsen and Nicolas Guégan, *"Associations: le tour de passe-passe d'Anne Hidalgo," Le Point*, October 23, 2015, www.lepoint.fr/politique/associations-le-tour-de-passe-passe-d-anne-hidalgo-23-10-2015-1976118_20.php#xtor=CS2-239.

It should be noted that no reimbursement, justification, or proper follow-up is required in exchange for the public money that is given away. They're full-on blank checks.[5] Hence many associations, which are supposed to be *associations sans but lucratif*—organizations whose point is not to make money (i.e., nonprofits)—end up becoming *associations lucratives sans but*—moneyed organizations that have no point!

But, hey . . . France is a country with a vision—one that insists on telling people what to do and think. Thus the eligibility criteria are widened to include those who:

- are interested in a cause that can help restrict civil liberties, such as freedom of speech.
- are unquestioning devotees of political correctness.
- want to inform French people of how racist they truly are deep inside.

Typically, *"les associations antiracistes"* (that is an actual phrase in France) gloriously tick these last three boxes: jackpot! Not only are they flooded with public money, but they also boast media coverage and political clout that are staggeringly disproportionate to the number of people who actually support them.[6] It makes you wonder ultimately who controls whom . . . which is pointless questioning, really—and simply goes to show that you are not in on it. It gets even better when you find out that the founder of one of these organizations turned Socialist Party apparatchik bought himself a $40,000 luxury watch

---

5 *"Subventions à Wattignies: manque de transparence?," La Voix du Nord*, May 23, 2014, www.lavoix dunord.fr/region/subventions-a-wattignies-manque-de-transparence-ia25b50462n2157846.

6 Eighty-six percent of French people are not interested in their activities and 70 percent view them as inefficient. *"Les Français contre le racisme . . . et les associations antiracistes," L'Express*, October 10, 2013, www.lexpress.fr/actualite/societe/les-francais-contre-le-racisme-et-les-associations -antiracistes_1288608.html.
Fabrice Durtal, *"SOS Racisme ou la dictature des potes," Contribuables Associés*, May 20, 2014, www .contribuables.org/2014/05/sos-racisme-ou-la-dictature-des-potes/.

(befitting a true socialist, obviously), and paid for more than half of it . . . in cash![7] Not shady at all!

In a country where the scope, the power, and the weight of government is already so dramatic, this system establishes a second public sector, as shadowy and illegitimate as it gets.

Needless to say, the few *associations* that denounce and oppose that system are not getting their share.

Useful tip: Volunteering in French is referred to as *faire du bénévolat*.

Sound like a French person: *"Il y a une vraie vie associative dans le quartier."* (This area is teeming with charitable organizations.)

7 Laurent Chabrun and Jean-Marie Pontaut, *"Julien Dray et sa montre 'à complication,'"* *L'Express*, December 9, 1999, www.lexpress.fr/informations/julien-dray-et-sa-montre-a-complication_636000.html.

NE PAS SE PRENDRE LA TÊTE

A phrase most students of French learn quickly when traveling to France is *ne pas se prendre la tête*. While relatively new, this expression has become a signature phrase among French people over the past two decades.

Literally, it translates as "not to take one's own head." What it means: "not to overthink it; not to worry about it too much." Someone who *se prend la tête* overthinks things. The implication is that such a person is missing out on life, fun, and laughter.

Ne te prends pas la tête is used in various settings and for various purposes:

- **At work:** Keep it simple and straightforward; don't overdo it!
- **Love life:** Your boyfriend or girlfriend is not worth your getting so upset!
- **General lifestyle:** Go the easy way; don't overcomplicate things.

Surely, a recommendation that consists of picking the easy way out of things has got to lead to some outstanding outcomes.

People are very quick these days at unholstering *se prendre la tête* and using it to (dis)qualify anyone who still goes through the trouble of using his brain. To many, if you're thinking, you've got to be over-thinking.

Useful tip: Rest assured, most French people are still quite good at *se prendre la tête*!

Sound like a French person: *"Te prends pas la tête, ça va aller!"* (Don't harp on it; it'll be fine!)

LA LAÏCITÉ

There is no understanding France these days if you don't have a good grasp of the term *laïcité*.

La laïcité refers to the separation of church and state. The French state is—to its very core—*laïc*, or secular. Just consider the fact that the first article (not the second!) of the French constitution defines France as a secular republic. In short, in France, religion should be a private matter, one that does not belong in public affairs. The general understanding is: "You have your faith; I have mine; this guy does not have any—and it's all good and well." This neutrality toward religion is meant to open the door to peaceful cohabitation and the triumph of reason.

Now, going back a few centuries, France was a deeply Catholic country. Today, it is probably one of the least religious countries in the world. This change was carefully crafted, primarily in Masonic Lodges, and implemented, for centuries, through the influence of Masons.

The French Revolution took care of the material takeover of a new class (riches were passed on from the nobility to the bourgeoisie), but the revolution could not be complete without also a deep change in the spiritual identity of the people. In short, to let go of the old France, you had to run Catholicism to the ground. The tool used to achieve that was *la laïcité*.[1]

Generation after generation, politicians made it clear and vocal that their allegiance was to *laïcité*. These politicians made it part of their mission to communicate this to the French people. The term *laïcard* appeared in the vernacular to designate this type of vindictive, religion-hating politician. The violence of this historical, spiritual, and political process is hard to fathom these days, especially in what has vastly become a postreligious country.

Undoubtedly, Masonry has won the battle against the Catholic Church in France. *La laïcité* is now essentially the new French organized religion.

Interestingly enough, the mass immigration of the past decades has brought about a new enemy to the sycophants of *laïcité*: Islam. Just when they thought the battle against God, transcendence, revelation, and a respect for traditional values had been won, a new nemesis surfaced in France. God was back!

Just as it was with the Catholics a few decades earlier, it is now the Muslims' turn to find out that, in France, secularism is the name of the game. In 2004, most of the world was shocked to find out about a law preventing Muslim schoolgirls from being veiled in school. That's *laïcité* for you. Though pious people in France and overseas struggle to understand and accept it, the values and the laws of the French Republic take precedence over those of any religion.

Some observers see a form of closed-mindedness in it. What most fail to realize is that what is at stake is not just keeping religion separate from government—it is the very confrontation of two religions: one official, one covert.

Faced with the growing influence of Islam, in 2010 the French

---

1 Vincent Peillon, French politician and onetime education minister: *Cette laïcité qui naît dans les loges . . . va d'abord apparaître comme une religion laïque: religion contre la religion catholique.*"

Republic controversially passed another law making it illegal to wear the niqab or burqa in public.

The French political class finds itself in an amusingly schizophrenic situation in which it promotes mass immigration of Muslim populations into France while simultaneously designating Islam as a potential peril to "the values of the republic." No doubt about it: the battle between the secular French Republic and Islam will be one of the defining battles of the upcoming decades in France. Neither will go down without a fight.

So much for the people who believed that *laïcité* meant peaceful cohabitation and the triumph of reason.

Useful tip: Except for practicing religious people, most citizens of France are big fans of *laïcité*.

Sound like a French person: *"La laïcité est au coeur de la culture française."* (Secularism is central to French culture.)

FIRST NAMES

$\mathcal{T}$hese days, expecting parents in France like to cultivate mystery. While it has grown very mainstream not to reveal the sex of the future child before the big day (*"On veut garder la surprise"*—We want to keep it a surprise), many parents have recently established a new level of secrecy. It concerns the first name.

No level of security clearance shall land you that crucial piece of information. Once the decision has been made to keep it a secret, it does not matter how close you are to one or both of the parents—you're with the rest of the punks, left clueless faced with this unfathomable and consuming question.

For these parents, one thing is not an option: for their baby's name to be stolen or mocked before the day he or she is born. Once the baby is born, basic courtesy will force any snide comments about the name to be made mostly behind the new parents' backs. As for stealing that one precious and carefully selected name: no longer an option, sucker!

Though many French parents like to create a reality-TV-like buildup before the revelation of their child's name, there's a good chance you can simply guess it. French names tend to come in waves of popularity. And no matter how desperately unique the young parents are trying to be, they will only find out a few years later when the child starts going to school—what? There are three other Lucases in your class! Bummer!

The rules of name giving are no longer family rules in France. The days are long gone where most names given to newborns were chosen among a short list of names that ran in the family as a tribute to parents, grandparents, or other important family members.

Every two or three years, new French favorites appear: sources of inspiration vary, but top ones undoubtedly include celebrities (Enzo, a leading boy's name in the 2000s, was the name soccer superstar Zinédine Zidane gave his first son) and ones related to movies or good old TV shows (Thierry, a sixties classic, was popularized by the show *Thierry La Fronde*).

The Most Commonly Given First Names Per Decade[1]

1950s	Marie, Martine	Jean, Philippe
1960s	Sylvie, Nathalie	Thierry, Christophe
1970s	Sandrine, Stéphanie, Céline	Stéphane, Sébastien
1980s	Aurélie, Émilie, Julie, Élodie	Nicolas, Julien
1990s	Marine, Manon	Kévin, Thomas
2000s	Léa, Emma	Lucas, Enzo

In the early nineties there was a massive surge in the popularity of American names in France. Not just any American names, but names straight out of popular American sitcoms. All the favorite characters were represented. Dylan, Brandon, or Brenda, for instance—all extremely popular in the early nineties—came straight from *Beverly Hills 90210*. Truthfully, why honor a family member when you could honor Brenda Walsh?

Unsurprisingly, those parents finding inspiration for their children's names in cheesy TV shows were usually of modest means and not particularly educated. Twenty years after this fad, people bearing Amer-

---

1 Alexandre Léchenet, *"Quels sont les prénoms les plus populaires depuis 1946,"* Le Monde, April 29, 2014, www.lemonde.fr/les-decodeurs/article/2014/04/29/la-carte-des-prenoms-les-plus -donnes-en-france_4408677_4355770.html#.

ican first names are still the butt of many jokes. Their first name, it's understood, is *un prénom de merde*—a crappy one. The good news: if the result of the 2012 London Olympics is any indication, it seems that mockery can be a good source of motivation in life. Indeed, French medalists bore first names such as Teddy, Tony, Bryan, Kévin (notice the accent), Mickael, Hamilton, or Steeve!

It should be noted at this point that there is not a chance in the world that your typical English speaker would ever recognize any of these names when pronounced the French way.

The floodgates to the endless world of *prénoms de merde* were opened in the 1990s, leaving our world with conversations about such names that—no matter how repetitive they may seem—are always entertaining. Some recent French favorites include a Burgundy couple naming their daughters Djaysie and Rihanna (the parents' names were Cynthia and Steven). And don't forget little Barack Obama (that's his first name) who was born in Normandy in 2015.[2] *That* birth certificate can be consulted easily.

One thing's for sure at this point: following French athletes in the coming years should get more and more interesting!

Useful tip: The vast majority of people bearing a double name starting with "Jean-" were born before the sixties.

Sound like a French person: *"Je déteste ce prénom!"* (I hate that name!)

---

2 *"Barack Obama, né à Évreux," Paris Normandie*, March 25, 2015, www.paris-normandie.fr/detail _article/articles/2819635/actualites+societe/barack-obama-ne-a-evreux#.VSRehbrBFFL.

NOT GETTING RICH

The saying goes that France is the worst country to make money in, but the best one to spend it in. While France makes it difficult to make money, it also specializes in making it very challenging to conserve it.

Consequently, a crucial difference between France and most other countries in the world lies in the fact that, in France, you'll find very few people sitting on a very large stack of cash. Savings and generational wealth are almost unheard-of in France. The confiscatory nature of the French fiscal system implemented over the past decades has had drastic consequences:

- **Number 1:** Rich people flee France and its ever-so-greedy tax man. A few hundred of the wealthiest families in France have been leaving the country each year. Needless to say, when they go, they take their money—or what's left of it—with them.

- **Number 2:** Many entrepreneurs also leave France when it comes time to sell their businesses, simply to avoid the fruits of their labors being taxed for the umpteenth time.

- **Number 3:** Professions that traditionally call for higher wages (medicine, law) are subject to high taxation and/or a socialized system—not preventing those professionals from leading a comfortable life, but limiting their ability to ever build up actual wealth.

- **Number 4:** If, by some ungodly miracle, by the end of your life the disgusting capitalist that you are managed to pay up in full one or two mortgages, you might end up owning a bit of real estate. Should you have the evil temptation of wanting to pass those goods to your children, you will again prove to the world that you are not a good socialist. Why would you want to give an advantage to your children? Heavy taxation shall apply. When you die, your children will have to pay up to 45 percent of the value of what gets passed on to them, which has forced millions to sell their parents' property in order to settle the payment of that tax. French tax man: always classy! For any donation you wish to make to a friend, a neighbor, a godchild, or a cousin, the rate goes up to 60 percent.[1] Ultimately, the main beneficiary of anyone's will in France is most likely the government. According to the dominant French socialist rhetoric, all children should be born in the same predicament (crap, that is).

Add the fact that, in their first years, French companies typically serve primarily a relatively small domestic market (65 million people vs. 320 million in the U.S.), and the money generated tends to be proportionally less than in larger countries.

If you aggregate all these factors, the direct consequence is a country with an ever-vanishing class of wealthy people, one that has typically grown quite leery of French authorities and consequently is rarely keen to invest in France.

More important, *les riches* are viewed by many in France as walking

---

1 *Observatoire des Gaspillages*, November 20, 2012, www.observatoiredesgaspillages.com/2012/11 /le-scandale-des-droits-de-succession-sans-lien-de-parente/.

stashes of cash in need of fiscal penalizing. François Hollande had no problem going on French TV and declaring, *"Je n'aime pas les riches"* (I don't like rich people). By *les riches*, he meant people earning more than €4,000 per month! Should you earn more than this, you're on our president's naughty list! Hollande's characterization of those earning €4,000 per month as "rich" is indicative of the general penchant of many French people to view the slightly less poor as the rich.

Financial success in France is not encouraged, it is very difficult to achieve, and, when it is, it is penalized and becomes the subject of finger-pointing.

In France, taxing the rich is viewed by millions as not only morally just, but also economically constructive. The idea of private investment in small companies is so remote from the general financial and ideological scope of most French people that it does not cross their collective mind as a key success factor for an economy. More money for the government surely works better!

Strangely, in a country where the government employs more than 25 percent of the workforce, they do—one must admit—have a point.

Useful tip: France is indeed a great place to spend money.

Sound like a French person: *"Et l'appartement du Boulevard Beaumarchais, du coup, c'est ta soeur qui l'a gardé? Bah non, on a dû le vendre."* (What about the Boulevard Beaumarchais apartment? Did your sister get it? Well, no, we had to sell it.)

FAST FOOD

France is now home to 1,285 McDonald's restaurants (affectionately dubbed "McDo").[1] Every day 1.8 million McDonald's meals are served in a country with a total population of approximately 66 million people. In terms of density, this means that France has 70 percent more McDonald's restaurants per square meter than the United States.

I hear Francophiles lament: *"But WHY? France has such great food—why would anyone eat at McDonald's?"*

The answer is simple: if you want to have a warm meal, enjoy Wi-Fi, sit down, and spend less than eight or nine euros for it, you hardly have a choice in France.

The culture of fast food in France has grown absolutely massive. And the Golden Arches is not the only player on this market. More than ten thousand kebab restaurants sprinkle the French territory. Plus, of course, the countless boulangeries that have expanded their traditional bread and pastries offer to include sandwiches and *formules midi* (lunch menu), which are set lunch deals generally consisting of a sandwich, a drink, and a pastry.

---

1 *"Nos Chiffres,"* McDonald's Web site, December 2013, www.mcdonalds.fr/en/entreprise/entreprise/qui-sommes-nous/chiffres.

As much as foreigners like to think of French people taking hours off and drinking profuse amounts of wine for lunch, that has become a rarity. The average amount of time French people dedicate to lunch is thirty-one minutes, and the average amount of money spent: €7.20 (which won't exactly get you a feast and multiple bottles of wine).[2] In 2012, the fast-food industry was a €34 billion market in France, thus accounting for 54 percent of its total restaurant business.

Simply put, in France these days, fast food is simply more popular than traditional restaurants.

Useful tip: When in France, do yourself a favor and avoid fast food. There are so many better options!

Sound like a French person: *"On se fait un McDo?"* (Wanna go to McDonald's?)

2 Audrey Avesque, *"McDo, kebab, sandwich . . . comment la restauration rapide a conquis la France,"* *L'Expansion,* March 1, 2013, http://lexpansion.lexpress.fr/actualite-economique/mcdo-kebab -sandwich-comment-la-restauration-rapide-a-conquis-la-fran ce_1437940.html.

SLOW FOOD

Thankfully enough, France is still home to thousands of lovely restaurants. And with (allegedly) food-loving Frenchies and millions of tourists streaming into the country in search of some French food, you would think that business would be good for most French restaurateurs.

You would be wrong.

In 2013, every day three new restaurants opened their doors in Paris (which happens to be not only the richest city in France, but also the most touristed city in the world), but, in that same day, five went out of business. This means that every single day Paris lost two restaurants.[1]

Now, what about outside Paris, then? Well, outside Paris, France is well-known for its numerous bistros, cafés, bars, and brasseries. Those have been shutting down at a rate of six per day over the past few years.[2] While in 1960 France boasted over two hundred thousand of these places of *convivialité*, we're down to a little more than thirty thousand.

1 Claire Bouleau, *"Chaque jour, Paris perd deux restaurants," Challenges,* July 8, 2014, www.challenges .fr/entreprise/20140630.CHA5598/pourquoi-chaque-jour-deux-restaurants-disparaissent-a-paris .html.
2 *"La France a perdu 2000 cafés en 2008," Le Figaro,* May 29, 2009, www.lefigaro.fr/flash-actu/2009 /05/29/01011-20090529FILWWW00428-la-france-a-perdu-2000-cafes-en-2008.php.

While it requires a prosperous population for a country to sustain its restaurant-scene excellence, it does not have to be that way at home. At home, anyone can cook great food: all it requires is time, money, and interest. In a typical French household, weekday meals differ from weekend meals. Weekday meals are rather simple (think salad, pasta, cheese or yogurt, bread, and a piece of fruit), and the French do also love their frozen food—the market for savory frozen food is worth €3.5 billion![3] On weekends, Saturday is typically a ramp-up day leading to the crowning meal of the French food week: Sunday lunch. Traditionally, French families gather for lunch on Sunday and treat themselves to a nice (and frequently long) meal. In Paris, where many yuppies don't have a family of their own or live far from them, the family *déjeuner du dimanche* has been supplanted by brunch with friends. Interestingly enough, Sunday brunch in France does not have the same boozy connotation it does in the Anglo world!

Now, you may wonder: what are the three most popular foods in France? Thinking *steak-frites*, *cassoulet*, and *magret de canard*? Try pasta, sandwiches, and pizza (in that order). Funnily enough, two of the three foods the French consume the most are originally Italian. To give you an idea, two million pizzas (typically frozen) are consumed each day in France. In the world, only Americans eat more pizza than the French. In fact, the French eat more pizza (per capita and in total) than the Italians!

On the good-news front, the rise of international cooking shows (*Top Chef*, *MasterChef*) has fueled new interest in food over the past few years. The encouraging change in the perception of organic food is also a very positive element. But while there are promising changes, if you want to understand the French food culture today, one thing is for sure: for most French people, it has much more to do with pizza, kebabs, and burgers than it does with superior gastronomy.

---

3 Yves Puget, "*Plats cuisinés surgelés: les chiffres du marché,*" *LSA Commerce & Consommation,* February 10, 2013, www.lsa-conso.fr/plats-cuisines-surgeles-les-chiffres-du-marche,138394.

Useful tip: When picking a restaurant, always make sure there are a few stickers saying the place was recommended by some guidebooks (even if those guidebooks don't sound familiar to you). It's a great way to maximize the odds of finding a small gem.

Sound like a French person: *"Tous les ans, j'achète mon vin d'un petit propriétaire. Dé-li-cieux!"* (Every year, I buy my wine from a small winemaker. De-li-cious!)

THE PRESS

$\mathcal{F}$rench press is not just a tool to make coffee. It's also a term that designates a number of virtually bankrupt media companies surviving primarily thanks to government subsidies.

Now, saying the French government controls the press simply because it gives over half a billion euros each year to French media outlets would be a tad excessive, wouldn't it?[1]

A more correct statement would therefore be that the French government, along with corporate interests, control the press in France. See, maybe the defense contractor that owns *Le Figaro* (Groupe Dassault—care for a fighter jet, anyone?) has an interest in France going to war, but the party in office doesn't. Now, that's a relief: checks and balances. That's what a real democracy is about. Freedom, baby!

Sadly, most French people don't like to take that step back and look into who's paying and who's benefiting. Granted, they're not exactly encouraged to do so when they turn on their TV or open up their newspaper. Consequently, most stick comfortably to the reassuring view that some publications are *super à droite* (very right-wing) while

---

1 Alexis Vintray, *"Aides à la presse: les chiffres," Contrepoints,* October 26, 2012, www.contrepoints
.org/2012/10/26/102090-subventions-aides-presse-les-chiffres.

others are *vachement à gauche* (very left-wing). Left, right, right, left: the soothing narrative of Western democracies is alive and well in France. Left ... right ... right ... left ... Marching mindlessly forward.

A wonderful homage to the undying French common sense, however, is the constant collapse in sales figures of all French newspapers and magazines. Little by little, more and more French people are starting to sense that, partial report after partial report, biased story after biased story, fabrication after fabrication, distraction after distraction, the world depicted by their favorite journalists is not quite congruent with the one they seem to live in. So they slowly stop spending their money to be dis- or misinformed. Most don't even think about it. It just happens. Loss of interest.

But these uninterested citizens are not going to be let off the hook that easily. Even if they don't buy magazines or newspapers, TV is still keen to help French people with their thinking. And once again, your remarkably involved French state is never far, operating in full nothing less than eleven TV channels.[2] Should you decide to turn off your TV, you'll still have to dodge the hundred-plus state-controlled radio stations.[3] Fun fact? Only China has more state-controlled and -sponsored media than France.[4]

The void left by the growing disconnect between what the French now call *les médias mainstream* and the general public is slowly but surely being filled, in France like in most Western countries, by a number of alternative media outlets. It's a very thrilling phenomenon to witness a growing fraction of the population making an active decision not to

---

2 Groupe France Télévisions operates France 2, France 3, France 4, France 5, France Ô, Outre-Mer 1ère, Public Sénat, and La chaîne parlementaire–Assemblée Nationale.

3 Groupe Radio France operates France Inter, France Info, and France Culture, which are the main ones pushing an agenda full-time. Its other stations are also interested in music: France Musique, FIP (a personal favorite), Mouv', and France Bleue.

4 Thibault Doidy de Kerguelen, *"Le bureau du Sénat refuse de fusionner sa chaîne de TV avec celle de l'Assemblée pour faire des économies . . . ," Ma Vie Mon Argent,* January 25, 2015, http://maviemonargent .info/le-senat-aime-gaspiller-largent-des-contribuables/.

listen to corporate- or state-controlled media (amusingly dubbed *les merdias,* a pun on *merde,* "crap," and *média*) and instead turn to investigative journalism and grassroots movements.

If you want to read more alternative media, here are a few names worth looking into:

In French:

cercledesvolontaires.fr, metatv.org, agenceinfolibre.fr, lesmouton senrages.fr, latelelibre.fr, jovanovic.com, tvlibertes.com, lesbrind herbes.org, preuves-par-images.fr, informaction.info, voltairenet .org, claireseveracrebellion.com, egaliteetreconciliation.fr, lelibre penseur.org

In English:

vigilantcitizen.com, drudgereport.com, presstv.ir, boilingfrogs post.com, wearechange.org

As the audience of these sites grows, discussions on- and off-line evolve. New elements get discussed; new questions are posed. The official historical, social, and political narratives are trembling under the weight and significance of this renewed discourse. Consequently, in France, like in most Western countries, freedom of speech and anonymity online are being attacked by lawmakers. It was recently made fully lawful for the government to spy on its citizens.[5] Rest assured, though: it is for our own good. Who needs free press, privacy, critical thinking, and open discussions anyway?

---

5 Marc Rees, *"Loi Renseignement: la liste impressionnante des services autorisés à surveiller,"* Next Inpact, December 14, 2015.

Jean-Claude Paye, *"Société de surveillance ou société surmoïque?,"* Égalité et Réconciliation, December 2, 2015, www.egaliteetreconciliation.fr/Societe-de-surveillance-ou-societe-surmoique-36454.html.

Useful tip: The no-news diet is very much worth trying.

Sound like a French person: *"Je regarde quasiment plus la télé, ils me tapent sur le système, tous!"* (I almost never watch TV anymore . . . can't stand that whole crowd anymore!)

LA CHANSON FRANÇAISE

When referring to *les grands chanteurs français*—France's great singers—two names come to mind: Jacques Brel and Georges Brassens, collectively known as "Brel et Brassens." Some would add a third name to that prestigious hall of fame: Léo Ferré, known simply as Ferré.

Jacques Brel (who was actually Belgian), Georges Brassens, and Léo Ferré indeed embody the highest level of this most French of traditions. Which tradition is that? In short, a tradition of sung poetry, where eminently talented lyricists compose timeless texts that strive to touch the souls of the people, reaching beyond social and cultural differences to gracefully narrate the joys, doubts, and sorrows of the human condition. *La génération des Brel, Brassens, Ferré,* as it's often referred to, was a beautiful gift to all French speakers after the tragedies of World War II. To this day, nobody has surpassed these masters, who remain admired by most.

Care to listen to these masters and their contemporaries? Just check them out on YouTube:

"La chanson des vieux amants" by Jacques Brel
"Chanson pour l'Auvergnat" by George Brassens

"Avec le temps" by Léo Ferré
"Le métèque" by George Moustaki
"Ma plus belle histoire d'amour" by Barbara

In the late 1970s and the 1980s, a new generation of French singers came to life, among them Michel Sardou, Alain Souchon, Laurent Voulzy, Michel Berger, and Julien Clerc. While the artists of the previous generation were the full package—fantastic writers, great melodists, and touching performers—these newcomers typically had only one or two of these talents. Their hits remain well-known pop songs in France to this day and countless baby boomer ladies still view these men as irresistibly charming.

Check these out on YouTube:

"Foule sentimentale" by Alain Souchon
"Je vole" by Michel Sardou
"Femmes, je vous aime" by Julien Clerc

The 1990s saw the birth of a new movement referred to as *la nouvelle chanson française*—the new French song. Like any musical movement, it has both fans and detractors. Chatting about music with French people, you will most likely witness someone erupt at some point:

Ah, Vincent Delerm, j'peux pas l'blairer, putain. Il sait pas chanter. C'est insupportable.

Argh, Vincent Delerm—I can't stand that guy. He can't even sing. I hate it.

This generation is indeed not characterized by vocal prowess. Your shy fourteen-year-old nephew with his uncertain changing voice would probably own a "singer" like Benjamin Biolay. Any karaoke night, any song. Bring it!

Benjamin, stop trying to look melancholic—you're about to get owned by a fourteen-year-old.

The men in this generation of artists do not exactly scream testosterone. But if the sensitive, puny, doubt-ridden, wondering French type is your thing, then you're in luck. When compared with the illustrious generation of postwar forefathers, most French people would agree that there is one who can genuinely, if not rival, at least remind them of the greats: Renan Luce.

Check these singers out on YouTube:

"Quatrième de couverture" by Vincent Delerm
"Je suis de celles" by Bénabar
"Des ménagements" by Aldebert
"Je suis une feuille" by Renan Luce

Since it is so focused on lyrics, the tradition of *la chanson française* may be somewhat lost on most foreigners, who simply reckon that French music is just as bad as French wine is good. Fair enough.

When it comes to comparing musical traditions, the general understanding in France is that:

L'anglais est quand même vachement plus musical comme langue.

English is actually much more musical a language—no question about it.

Then, if you're in luck, somebody will end the conversation with a jab:

Ouais, parce que si tu traduis les paroles des chansons en anglais, tu pleures. Même les Beatles: "Yellow Submarine" . . . Putain, mais ça fait, "On vit tous dans un grand sous-marin jaune, grand sous-marin jaune . . ." Sérieusement, ça vole pas très haut.

Yeah, 'cause if you translate the lyrics of songs written in English, it's disastrous. Even the Beatles: "We all live in a yellow submarine . . ." Seriously, not exactly impressive stuff.

In an effort to share some of the best *chansons* in French or by French or French-speaking artists of recent years, I've taken the liberty of compiling a list of personal recommendations for your personal enjoyment. If you look them up on YouTube, simply prepare to witness serious puniness:

2000s:

"Formidable" by Stromae
"Mec à la cool" by Manu Larrouy
"Elisa" by Volo
"Salut marin" by Carla Bruni
"Souvenir de ma mère" by Gordon Sanchez
"De cap tà l'immortèla" by Nadau
"Midi 20" by Grand Corps Malade
"Hip Hop" by Hocus Pocus (featuring Procussions)
"L'homme du moment" by Alexis HK
"T'es beau" by Pauline Croze
"Mama Sam" by M
"Dans 150 ans" by Raphaël
"Belle à en crever" by Olivia Ruiz
"Shaünipul" by Nosfell
"La ferme" by Les Fatals Picards
"Les limites" by Julien Doré
"La vida tombola" by Manu Chao

1990s:

"Vous avez l'heure?" by Louise Attaque
"Les yeux de ma mère" by Arno
"Out of Time Man" by Mano Negra

1980s:

"La médaille" by Renaud

"Avoir et être" by Yves Duteil

"Quelque chose de Tennessee" by Johnny Hallyday

"Je suis venu te dire" by Serge Gainsbourg

"Les corons" by Pierre Bachelet

1970s:

"Les gens qui doutent" by Anne Sylvestre

"Mon vieux" by Daniel Guichard

"Mon frère" by Maxime Le Forestier

"Lily" by Pierre Perret

"Il est libre Max" by Hervé Cristiani

1960s:

"Nathalie" by Gilbert Bécaud

"Aragon et Castille" by Boby Lapointe

"Milord" by Édith Piaf

"La Tendresse" by Bourvil

Useful tip: Did you know that Manu Chao is actually French?

Sound like a French person: *"J'écoute un peu de tout."* (I listen to a bit of everything.)

RADARS

*T*ravel to New Orleans on Mardi Gras and you'll find an entire city filled with people asking to be flashed. Travel to France and you'll find an entire population railing against it.

For the verb *flasher* bears a very different meaning on this side of the pond. *Se faire flasher* means getting photographed and fined by a radar on the side of the road.

Not as fun.

When you drive in France, the odds of getting photographed and fined by a radar speed trap have increased exponentially over the past decade. A decade ago, radars were occasional affairs handled by cops, and getting caught was most likely both bad luck and well deserved.

Ever since, the French government decided to wage a very French war: an unlosable, enemyless war. A war in favor of safe driving.

Since the 1970s, the death toll on the road had been consistently dropping, due to the significant and continual improvements in the quality of cars, roads, first-aid responsiveness, air bags, road lighting, and so on. That trend was not going anywhere, and as technology progressed, numbers were bound to keep falling. That's when French politicians bravely decided to step in.

The opportunity of taking quality-of-life-blasting measures while manipulating the general public and finding that elusive chance to take credit for something that has absolutely nothing to do with you or your actions is a bit of a dream come true for a French politician.

You mean I can do all that at once?

Yup . . .

Man, I love my life!

Ten years later, the results of this policy are staggering:

- 4,200 automatic radar speed traps have been installed throughout France.[1]
- 13 million speeding tickets are sent in the mail each year.[2]
- 95 percent of them are for exceeding the speed limit by less than 12 miles per hour (20 kilometers per hour).[3]
- €800 million in fines (yes, that's close to a billion dollars) is collected each year.[4]

Any conversation about radars will lead to someone mentioning the phrase *pompes à fric* (money pumps). For while the project was well accepted at first, more and more French people are waking up to the fact that their government is indeed using radars not to improve their safety (surprise, surprise), but instead to rob them.

---

1 *"4200 radars d'ici la fin de l'année 2013,"* L'Express, June 21, 2013, www.lexpress.fr/actualite/societe/trafic/4200-radars-d-ici-la-fin-de-l-annee-2013_1259572.html.
2 *"Radars automatiques: nouveau record de contraventions,"* Le Monde, February 25, 2016, www.lemonde.fr/securite-routiere/article/2016/02/25/radars-automatiques-nouveau-record-de-contraventions_4871824_1655513.html.
3 *"Révélations fracassantes sur le business des radars en France,"* Économie Politique, May 30, 2013, http://economiepolitique.org/revelations-fracassantes-sur-le-business-des-radars/.
4 Stéphanie Fontaine, *"Les radars rapportent toujours plus à l'Etat,"* Caradisiac, October 8, 2013, www.caradisiac.com/Les-radars-rapportent-toujours-plus-a-l-Etat-89683.htm.

In France, you can be a perfectly safe driver, on a safe road, and get *flashé*—and therefore fined—if you're going one mile per hour over the limit. Never short of ideas to do its citizens wrong, the government even frequently lowers the speed limit right before the radar to trick and mislead drivers into oblivious speeding.[5] Effectively so: fifty-two of the top one hundred most profitable radars in France in 2013 were situated on roads where the speed limit had just been lowered, leading to up to four times the profitability.[6] New types of radars are constantly popping up: radars for red lights, radars for railroad crossings, double-faced radars, radars for stop signs, radars for safety distances, radars for average speed, etc.

Oh, the Orwellian toy set . . .

The most profitable radar in the country, near Annecy, catches close to five hundred people daily and generates over €20 million a year in profit.[7] Not a bad business model, one must admit!

In just a decade, driving a car (or a bike, or a truck, or a moped) in France has become not only a whole lot more stressful, but also a lot more expensive. The situation has gotten so bad that more and more French drivers are getting aggravated by this ultrarepressive policy. Not only is it costing them stress and money, but it's also a clear indication of the double standards of their government: harassing the average citizen on the road while cutting massive slack to actual criminals.

5 Jihane Bensouda, *"Ces radars qui nous piègent," Le Lynx*, April 29, 2013, www.lelynx.fr/assurance -auto/actualites/ces-radars-qui-nous-piegent-14498/.

6 *"Enquête: Radars: vitesse abaissée, rentabilité assurée!," Ligue de Défense des Conducteurs*, http://www .liguedesconducteurs.org/images/TOP%20100%20Radars%20tude.pdf.

7 Fabrice Amedeo, *"Le meilleur radar de France rapporte 22 millions par an," Le Figaro*, February 13, 2012, www.lefigaro.fr/actualite-france/2012/02/13/01016-20120213ARTFIG00380-le-meilleur -radar-de-france-rapporte-22-millions-par-an.php.

Useful tip: Be attentive!

Sound like a French person: *"J'me suis fait flasher à 52 au lieu de 50. C'est vraiment n'importe quoi. Tout est bon pour te faire cracher!"* (I got busted at 52 instead of 50 kilometers per hour. It truly is preposterous. Anything to make people pay!)

VDM

Over the past decade, one Web site has grown to become not only a well-known landmark of French pop culture, but also a new catchphrase in the French language. That Web site is simply called Vie de Merde. Translation: "The Crappy Life."

The site offers a collection of unfortunate anecdotes phrased in less than three hundred characters—thus offering a very telling reflection of the difference between France and America: Vie de Merde is twice as wordy as Twitter and focused exclusively on the negative. Being French is indeed a real *art de vivre* . . .

On the site, the most popular post of all time reads:

Aujourd'hui, je suis dans ma 45e année et je suis toujours puceau. VDM (Today, I'm 45 years old and I'm still a virgin. VDM)

Three thousand comments and over 1.5 million votes.

Yes, the French are people of great culture.

Undoubtedly, that person has grown to become the second most well-known virgin in the history of France, right after Joan of Arc.

The popularity of the site is staggering: while it receives over three thousand "VDM" submissions a day, only two or three make the cut and get published. For when it comes to describing how crappy life can be, the French are most demanding experts. *La crème de la crème de la crap!*

Interestingly, while the site's founders launched the concept in other countries, no nation has responded as well as France to the idea of a curated, funny site dedicated to the bad things that happen in life. Dwelling upon strangers' misfortunes is a pastime that, for some reason, other cultures on the planet don't relate to on a grand scale as something fun and relaxing.

The site now sells books and T-shirts and has even been turned into a TV show. VDM is a true French social phenomenon.

Now, should your mind venture to think that looking at a computer screen laughing at other people's misfortunes is equivalent in and of itself to a VDM, you're giving away one more clue that you are decidedly not that French, you cheeky thing!

Useful tip: Let's not forget that life is great!

Sound like a French person: *"L'autre, ses gamins lui parlent plus et sa femme s'est barrée: mais quelle vie de merde!"* (That guy . . . his kids won't speak to him, and his wife took off: what a crap life!)

PARALLEL
LANGUAGES

$\mathcal{T}$he French language is beautiful. Pity it's hardly spoken in France, for the language generally spoken by most French people is constantly sprinkled—if not smothered—with *argot*.

Argot is a parallel colloquial French language. It's the dark side of the force, the underground lingo. It's the French not taught in schools; it's passed on strictly orally, shaped and modified generation after generation. French speakers can easily distinguish proper French from *argot*. But many are simply oblivious to their irrepressible use of *argot* terms.

Whenever my fluent American wife joins a conversation involving only French speakers, I find myself translating a good half of the words spoken for her to be able to follow.

EXAMPLE 1:

- *Le mec bouffait dans sa bagnole.*
- *Dans la poubelle à côté du rade?*
- *Carrément. Il se faisait un McDo, pépère en tirant sur un bédo.*

Me: So, honey, they're talking about a man who was eating a takeaway meal from McDonald's while smoking a joint in his beat-up car that was parked right by a bar.

My wife: Hmm. Okay.

EXAMPLE 2:

- *J'me suis fait cramer par mon frangin.*
- *T'avais piqué le clebs de tes vieux pour une chouille?*
- *T'as eu de la moule qu'ils appellent pas les flics, putain!*

Me: Okay, so now my friend got busted by his brother after taking his parents' dog to a party, and they're saying he was lucky that the parents didn't call the cops.

My wife: Hmm. Okay.

Me (in petto): Note to self: Make friends that speak proper French or English.

But *argot* is not the only gray language used in France. *Verlan* is also there to confuse foreigners (and French people) even more. *Le verlan* is an urban dialect that vastly appeared in the 1980s in the *banlieues* as a means for kids to not be understood by police and those outside of their community, somewhat like pig latin, or gibberish.

While *argot* words must be learned, *verlan* words can be formed with a basic command of French. To form a word in *verlan*, take the original French word—for example, *voiture*, "car"—and invert the syllables: *turevoi*. If the resulting word ends with an unstressed vowel, drop it—so *photo* would become *topho*, and finally *toph*. This last rule is, in most instances, too complicated for most.

So let's go back to our examples. Depending on the group of friends

I am hanging out with, the conversation would lean less toward *argot*, more toward *verlan*:

EXAMPLE 1:

- *Le keumé était en train de géman dans sa turevoi.*
- *Dans la demer à côté du bar?*
- *Ouais, quiltran, en plus il méfu en se faisant son Do.*

EXAMPLE 2:

- *Mon reufré m'a cramé.*
- *T'avais péta le iench de tes remps pour une réssoi?*
- *T'as eu de la teuch qu'ils appellent pas les keufs, putain!*

Note that many words commonly used in *verlan* are based on *argot* words.

Sprinkle with the occasional Gypsy term (or Arabic in certain circles), the alternative *argot* synonym, and you're in for a language that resembles the one commonly spoken in French bars, factories, and streets:

EXAMPLE 1:

- *Le gadjo était en train de grailler dans sa caisse.*
- *Dans la daube à côté du trocson?*
- *Ouais, détendu du zguègue, il se fumait son oinj en plus.*

EXAMPLE 2:

- *J'me suis fait griller par mon frangin.*
- *T'avais chouravé le clébard de tes vieux?*
- *T'as le cul bordé de nouilles, putain. Il aurait pu appelé les kisdés.*

Who said learning French was difficult?

Useful tip: If you don't understand certain words spoken by French people, just ask!

Sound like a French person: *"Elle s'est fait la malle avec un rosbif."* (Literally: She packed her suitcase with a roast beef. In reality: She took off with a Brit.)

INTERMINABLE
GOOD-BYES

$\mathcal{I}$t is hard to distinguish whether the French are absolutely glorious or entirely catastrophic at good-byes. What is for sure, however, is that when planning to part company with French people socially, it is reasonable to anticipate anywhere between ten minutes and two hours for it.

It is therefore essential to time your first notice properly. Reasonably, a fair bit of time before you actually intend to leave.

Upon announcing that you have to go, a few scenarios may typically play out:

SCENARIO 1:

Everyone starts kissing good-bye. Systematically, one person pulls the ultimate French move: the untimely comment or question. Something like "It was great to see you. You look great. How's your mother, by the way?" Boom—ten-minute penalty.

Frequently, when two couples are parting ways, two separate conversations strike up at the time of good-byes. It is not rare for these conversations to be the most pleasant and the most meaningful of the interaction.

SCENARIO 2:

This scenario typically happens at the end of *une soirée arrosée*—literally, "a sprinkled evening," or a boozy night.

Okay. I have to run.

Come on—not already. It's super early.

At which point, the person about to be left will suggest one last drink or will play some form of emotional card to retain his friend's company for a little longer. It is helpful to realize that at that point both sides might be ready to go home. However, through a very twisted form of tipsy French politeness, one side will try to push back the parting time.

The key here: it's not at all rude for one friend to force the other to stay, but when that friend refuses to stay longer even if he has no interest in it—that's a tough one to come back from.

SCENARIO 3—AKA THE COUPLES SCENARIO:

In France, when a couple decides to leave a group of friends, man and woman typically say their good-byes separately. One of the two usually takes longer, either because he is less willing to take off or because she is subjected to more "stay pressure." At that point, the other anxious partner, in a brilliant time-management move, will engage in an entirely forced conversation with another person. The resulting exchange is a mere excuse to discreetly listen to the advancement of their significant other's progress.

Wanting to part ways is somehow generally interpreted as if the person wanting to leave would always rather be somewhere else. It never even occurs to the French that there are things like other obligations, exhaustion, or understanding that the time has simply come.

French good-byes are emotionally loaded: strangely, leaving always seems to mean *wanting* to leave but at the same time never *having* to leave. For that reason, French people typically try to get the leaver to stay longer, mainly to prove to him that their company is worthy and that the moment in their company does qualify as good times. The leaver's response generally consists of indulging others' attempts, for a part of him experiences the guilt of being that inconsiderate person who wants to be someplace else. Whether or not he does is irrelevant. The moment he started his good-byes, he knew full well the road to the door was also that to redemption.

Useful tip: Savor the awkwardness!

Sound like a French person: *"Non, vraiment, c'était génial. Faut absolument qu'on se refasse ça bientôt."* (Really, that was great. We should do it again soon.)

TRAVELING TO PARIS? LIKE WINE?

*I*f all went according to plan, you probably drank a few glasses of wine while reading this book. Good for you!

If you like wine and if you're not averse to a shameless plug, it would be my honor to recommend two places for your France/Paris to-do list. I have put lots of love and energy into them and truly think they both genuinely rock. Great places to learn, laugh, and drink good wine! Also, just present a picture of this page on your phone and your party will receive a 10 percent discount.

O Chateau

www.o-chateau.com

O Chateau offers wine-tasting classes and wine tours . . . and it's my favorite wine bar in Paris!

Les Caves du Louvre

www.cavesdulouvre.com

Winemaking workshops and enchanting sensory experiences in a royal wine cellar in central Paris.

See you soon!